Gretchen Bitterlin
Dennis Johnson
Donna Price
Sylvia Ramirez
K. Lynn Savage, Series Editor

Add Ventures 2
MULTILEVEL WORKSHEETS

with **Kathleen Olson**
Ingrid Wisniewska

CAMBRIDGE
UNIVERSITY PRESS

CAMBRIDGE UNIVERSITY PRESS
Cambridge, New York, Melbourne, Madrid, Cape Town, Singapore,
São Paulo, Delhi, Dubai Tokyo, Mexico City

Cambridge University Press
32 Avenue of the Americas, New York, NY 10013–2473, USA

www.cambridge.org
Information on this title: www.cambridge.org/9780521675840

First published 2008
4th printing 2010

Printed in the United States of America

A catalog record for this publication is available from the British Library.

ISBN 978-0-521-54839-7 pack consisting of Student's Book and Audio CD
ISBN 978-0-521-67959-6 Workbook
ISBN 978-0-521-69080-5 pack consisting of Teacher's Edition and Teacher's Toolkit Audio CD / CD-ROM
ISBN 978-0-521-67728-8 CDs (Audio)
ISBN 978-0-521-67729-5 Cassettes
ISBN 978-0-521-67584-0 Add Ventures

Art direction, book design, photo research, and layout services: Adventure House, NYC
Layout services: TSI Graphics, Effingham, IL

Contents

Introduction

What is *Add Ventures*?

Add Ventures 2 is a book of reproducible worksheets to accompany the **Ventures** Student's Book 2. The worksheets give students additional practice for each lesson in the Student's Book at three levels of difficulty, making it the ideal supplemental material for multilevel classrooms.

For each two-page lesson in the Student's Book, there are three *Add Ventures* worksheets. Each worksheet is designed to provide up to 30 minutes of student work.

What are the three levels of difficulty in *Add Ventures*?

The three tiers in *Add Ventures* allow students who are in the same class but at different levels of English ability to gain confidence and proficiency through level-appropriate tasks.

☑ ■ ■ Tier 1 tasks are controlled exercises targeted at students who need the most support as they progress through the Student's Book. A major goal of Tier 1 tasks is to build students' confidence as they work.

■ ☑ ■ Tier 2 tasks target students for whom the level of the Student's Book is just right. The exercises are similar to those in the main text. The goal of Tier 2 is to provide additional on-level practice.

■ ■ ☑ Tier 3 tasks provide the least support and the greatest challenge. They require more production with fewer cues, and they may extend the content of the lesson in the Student's Book. These tasks target students who move quickly and can easily make connections with previously learned content. The goal of Tier 3 is to challenge students beyond the tasks in the Student's Book.

How do I use *Add Ventures*?

The three tiers of tasks can be structured for *like-ability* (homogeneous) or *cross-ability* (heterogeneous) groups.

In like-ability groupings, students at the *same ability level* work on the same tasks. That is, those students needing the most support work together on Tier 1; students needing the least support work together on Tier 3; students needing more on-level practice work together on Tier 2.

The same or similar content in the tasks across the three tiers of each lesson makes correction easy. Teachers can bring the students together as a whole class to review the answers because the answers on the three worksheets are the same across the tiers.

In cross-ability groupings, students at *different ability levels* work together but use their own level worksheet. Strong students and less strong students work together, enabling peer teaching and peer correction. With cross-ability groupings, the class is usually divided into two groups rather than three. That is, Tier 3 students may work with Tier 1 students while Tier 2 students work in their like-ability group; or Tier 2 students may work with Tier 1 students while Tier 3 students work in their like-ability group. With this cross-ability grouping, feedback on tasks is most often done within the group (student-to-student) rather than as a whole-class activity.

How is *Add Ventures* different from the Workbook for *Ventures*?

The **Workbook** is designed for independent student use outside of class, although it can also be used as additional in-class practice. It provides reinforcement activities at the same level as the lessons in the Student's Book.

Add Ventures is intended for in-class use, particularly in multilevel settings, to target the exercises specific to a student's language-ability level.

Add Ventures worksheets can be used after each lesson in the Student's Book or in conjunction with the Workbook.

Use the Workbook exercises first to determine the appropriate tier of *Add Ventures* to assign to each student. Or use *Add Ventures* first to address individual needs of students prior to assigning the Workbook. In this case, determine the worksheet tier for each student based on the student's understanding of the material in the Student's Book. After successful completion of their *Add Ventures* worksheets, students can do the exercises in the Workbook, either as additional classroom practice or as homework.

A Look at the picture. Read the sentences. Write the names.

1. Lisa has long curly hair. She is wearing a striped shirt.

2. Bill has short straight hair. He is wearing black shoes.

3. Sue has short curly hair. She is wearing a black skirt.

4. Eva has long straight hair. She is wearing a black shirt.

5. José has short curly hair. He is wearing a soccer uniform.

B Look at the picture in Exercise A. Complete the sentences.

1. Ann has _____*short*_____ curly hair. She is wearing a black _____*shirt*_____ .
   (long / short)   (shirt / uniform)

2. Tom has _____ straight hair. He is wearing a _____ shirt.
   (long / short)   (black / striped)

3. Jim has short _____ hair. He is wearing a soccer _____ .
   (curly / straight)   (pants / uniform)

C Write sentences.

1. Describe your hair. _____

2. Describe your partner's hair. _____

Name: _____

Lesson A *Get ready*

A Look at the picture. Complete the sentences.

Lisa | José | Bill | Eva | Tom | Sue | Jim | Ann

| black | curly | long | shirt | short | skirt | straight | striped | uniform |

1. Lisa has long curly hair. She is wearing a _____*striped*_____ shirt.

2. Bill has short _____ hair. He is wearing _____ shoes.

3. Sue has short _____ hair. She is wearing a black _____ .

4. Eva has _____ straight hair. She is wearing a black _____ .

5. José has _____ curly hair. He is wearing a soccer _____ .

B Look at the picture in Exercise A. Complete the sentences.

| long | shirt | short | straight | striped | uniform |

1. Ann has _____*short*_____ curly hair. She is wearing a black _____*shirt*_____ .

2. Tom has _____ straight hair. He is wearing a _____ shirt.

3. Jim has short _____ hair. He is wearing a soccer _____ .

C Write sentences.

1. Describe your hair. _____

2. Describe your partner's hair. _____

3. Describe your teacher's hair. _____

Lesson A *Get ready*

Name: _____

A Look at the picture. Complete the sentences.

| Lisa | José | Bill | Eva | Tom | Sue | Jim | Ann |

1. Lisa has _____*long*_____ _____*curly*_____ hair. She is wearing a _____*striped*_____ shirt.

2. Bill has _____ _____ hair. He is wearing _____ shoes.

3. Sue has _____ _____ hair. She is wearing a black _____ .

4. Eva has _____ _____ hair. She is wearing a black _____ .

5. José has _____ _____ hair. He is wearing a _____ _____ .

B Look at the picture in Exercise A. Complete the sentences.

1. Ann has _____*short*_____ curly hair. She is wearing a black _____*shirt*_____ .

2. Tom has _____ straight hair. He is wearing a _____ shirt.

3. Jim has short _____ hair. He is wearing a soccer _____ .

C Write sentences.

1. Describe your hair. _____

2. Describe your partner's hair. _____

3. Describe your teacher's hair. _____

4. What are you wearing? _____

Name: _____

Lesson B *She's wearing a short plaid skirt.*

A Look at the pictures. Circle the answers.

1    **2**    **3**    **4**

a. small (b. large)	a. large b. small	a. long b. short	a. long b. small
(a. checked) b. striped	a. striped b. checked	a. striped b. plaid	a. checked b. striped
a. boots (b. pants)	a. suit b. shirt	a. sweater b. coat	a. socks b. pants

B Write the correct word.

1. a large _____*red*_____ backpack
   (red / small)

2. a _____ purple coat
   (green / small)

3. a black _____ skirt
   (long / plaid)

4. _____ striped socks
   (checked / green)

C Write the words in the correct order.

1. checked / large / a / shirt *a large checked shirt* _____

2. dress / short / black / a _____

3. small / sweater / a / blue _____

© Cambridge University Press 2008 **Photocopiable**

Lesson B *She's wearing a short plaid skirt.*

A Look at the pictures. Circle the answers.

❶  ❷  ❸  ❹

a. small	a. large	a. large	a. long
b. long	b. small	b. long	b. small
c. (large)	c. short	c. short	c. short
a. (checked)	a. striped	a. checked	a. checked
b. striped	b. plaid	b. striped	b. striped
c. plaid	c. checked	c. plaid	c. black
a. boots	a. suit	a. sweater	a. socks
b. (pants)	b. pants	b. coat	b. pants
c. skirt	c. shirt	c. skirt	c. skirt

B Write the words in the correct order.

1. a _____*large*_____ _____*red*_____ backpack
   (red / large)

2. a _____ _____ coat
   (purple / small)

3. a _____ _____ skirt
   (plaid / black)

4. _____ _____ socks
   (striped / green)

C Write the words in the correct order.

1. checked / large / a / shirt _____*a large checked shirt*_____

2. dress / short / black / a _____

3. small / sweater / a / blue _____

4. striped / pants / long _____

Name: _____

Lesson B *She's wearing a short plaid skirt.*

A Look at the pictures. Complete the chart.

 1
 2
 3
 4

Size: large			
Pattern: checked			
Clothing type: pants			

B Write the words in the correct order.

1. a _____*large*_____ _____*red*_____ backpack
   (large / red)

2. a _____ _____ coat
   (purple / small)

3. a _____ _____ skirt
   (plaid / black)

4. _____ _____ socks
   (striped / green)

C Write the words in the correct order.

1. checked / large / a / shirt *a large checked shirt*_____

2. dress / short / black / a _____

3. small / sweater / a / blue _____

4. striped / pants / long _____

5. suit / a small / plaid _____

6. boots / short / brown _____

Name: _____

Lesson C *What are you doing right now?*

A Look at the schedule. Complete the sentences.

	Eduardo	**Ivana**	**Lin**
Monday	watch TV	watch TV	watch TV
Tuesday	do homework		do homework
Wednesday	play soccer	clean the house	
Thursday	go to class	study English	clean the kitchen
Friday	call Ed		study English
Saturday			watch movies
Sunday	play soccer	call her mother	rest

are watching	is playing	is studying	plays	studies

1. Today is Wednesday. What is Eduardo doing now? Eduardo _____*is playing*_____ soccer.

2. What does Ivana do every Thursday? Ivana _____ English.

3. Today is Friday. What is Lin doing now? Lin _____ English.

4. What does Eduardo do on Sunday? Eduardo _____ soccer.

5. Today is Monday. What are Eduardo, Ivana, and Lin doing now?

   They _____ TV.

B Complete the conversations. Use the information from Exercise A.

1. **A** What _d_ _o_ _e_ _s_ Lin _d_ _o_ on Sunday?

   B She _r_ _e_ _s_ _t_ _s_ .

2. **A** What ___ ___ ___ ___ Eduardo ___ ___ on Thursday?

   B He ___ ___ ___ ___ ___ ___ ___ ___ ___ ___ ___ .

3. **A** What ___ ___ Eduardo and Lin ___ ___ on Tuesday?

   B They ___ ___ homework.

4. **A** Today is Wednesday. What ___ ___ Ivana ___ ___ ___ ___ ___ right now?

   B She ___ ___ ___ ___ ___ ___ ___ ___ ___ ___ the house.

C Answer the questions. Use your own information.

1. What are you doing now? _____

2. What do you always do in the morning? _____

Name: _____

Lesson C *What are you doing right now?*

A Look at the schedule. Complete the sentences.

	Eduardo	**Ivana**	**Lin**
Monday	watch TV	watch TV	watch TV
Tuesday	do homework	study English	do homework
Wednesday	play soccer	clean the house	
Thursday	go to class	study English	clean the kitchen
Friday	call Ed		study English
Saturday		watch movies	watch movies
Sunday	play soccer	call her mother	rest

1. Today is Wednesday. What is Eduardo doing now? Eduardo ____is____ ____playing____ soccer.

2. What does Ivana do every Thursday? Ivana _____ _____ .

3. Today is Friday. What is Lin doing now? Lin _____ _____ _____ .

4. What does Eduardo do on Sunday? Eduardo _____ _____ .

5. Today is Monday. What are Eduardo, Ivana, and Lin doing now?

   They _____ _____ TV.

B Complete the conversations. Use the information from Exercise A.

1. **A** What ____does____ Lin ____do____ on Sunday?

   B She ____rests____ .

2. **A** What _____ Eduardo _____ on Thursday?

   B He _____ _____ _____.

3. **A** What _____ Eduardo and Lin _____ on Tuesday?

   B They _____ _____ .

4. **A** Today is Wednesday. What _____ Ivana _____ right now?

   B She _____ _____ the house.

C Answer the questions. Use your own information.

1. What are you doing now? _____

2. What do you always do in the morning? _____

3. What do you usually do in the afternoon? _____

Name: _____

Lesson C *What are you doing right now?*

A Look at the schedule. Complete the sentences.

	Eduardo	**Ivana**	**Lin**
Monday	watch TV	watch TV	watch TV
Tuesday	do homework	study English	do homework
Wednesday	play soccer	clean the house	go to the park
Thursday	go to class	study English	clean the kitchen
Friday	call Ed	go to the library	study English
Saturday	go swimming	watch movies	watch movies
Sunday	play soccer	call her mother	rest

1. Today is Wednesday. What is Eduardo doing now? Eduardo *is playing soccer* .

2. What does Ivana do every Thursday? Ivana _____ .

3. Today is Friday. What is Lin doing now? Lin _____ .

4. What does Eduardo do on Sunday? Eduardo _____ .

5. Today is Monday. What are Eduardo, Ivana, and Lin doing now?

   They _____ .

B Complete the conversations. Use the information from Exercise A.

1. **A** What ____*does*____ Lin ____*do*____ on Sunday?

   B She ____*rests*____ .

2. **A** What _____ Eduardo _____ on Thursday?

   B He _____ .

3. **A** What _____ Eduardo and Lin _____ on Tuesday?

   B They _____ .

4. **A** Today is Wednesday. What _____ Ivana _____ right now?

   B She _____ .

C Answer the questions. Use your own information.

1. What are you doing now? _____

2. What do you always do in the morning? _____

3. What do you usually do in the afternoon? _____

4. What do you do every night? _____

Lesson D Reading

Name: _____

A Match the pictures with the words.

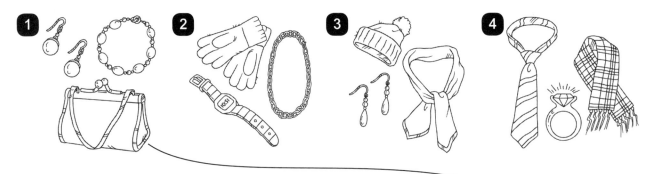

1 **2** **3** **4**

a. scarf, hat, earrings

b. ring, scarf, tie

c. watch, gloves, necklace

d. bracelet, earrings, purse

B Read Annie's letter. Circle the answers.

Dear Auntie Julia,

The last time you saw me, I was a teenager. I was a high school student, and I had long hair. Now I'm 20 years old, and I'm a student at the university. I study computers. I play soccer every week. I really like it here, and I have a lot of friends. We usually go hiking on the weekend. I'm sending you a picture of me at my school. I have short hair now, and I usually wear jeans. In this picture, I'm wearing a dress. I hope you like the picture.

Please come and visit me.

Love,
Annie

1. How old is Annie?   a. She's a teenager.   b. She's 20 years old.
2. What does she study?   a. sports   b. computers
3. When does she play soccer?   a. every week   b. on the weekend
4. When does she go hiking?   a. every week   b. on the weekend
5. What does she usually wear?   a. jeans   b. a dress
6. What is she wearing in the picture? a. jeans   b. a dress

Name: _____

Lesson D *Reading*

A Look at the pictures. Write the words. Use some words more than once.

bracelet	gloves	necklace	ring	tie
earrings	hat	purse	scarf	watch

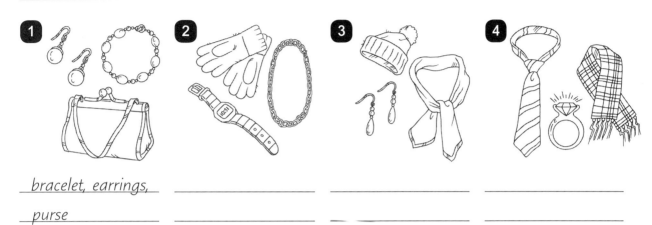

1 _____
   bracelet, earrings,
   purse

2 _____

3 _____

4 _____

B Read Annie's letter. Circle the answers.

Dear Auntie Julia,

   The last time you saw me, I was a teenager. I was a high school student, and I had long hair. Now I'm 20 years old, and I'm a student at the university. I study computers. I play soccer every week. I really like it here, and I have a lot of friends. We usually go hiking on the weekend. I'm sending you a picture of me at my school. I have short hair now, and I usually wear jeans. In this picture, I'm wearing a dress. I hope you like the picture.

Please come and visit me.

Love,
Annie

1. How old is Annie?   a. She's a teenager.   (b. She's 20 years old.)   c. She's a student.

2. What does she study?   a. hiking   b. computers   c. sports

3. When does she play   a. every week   b. on the weekend   c. at the university
   soccer?

4. When does she go   a. at school   b. every week   c. on the weekend
   hiking?

5. What does she usually   a. jeans   b. a dress   c. a skirt
   wear?

6. What is she wearing   a. jeans   b. a skirt   c. a dress
   in the picture?

Lesson D Reading

A Look at the pictures. Write the words.

1 **2** **3** **4**

bracelet, earrings, _____ _____ _____

purse _____ _____ _____

B Read Annie's letter. Answer the questions.

Dear Auntie Julia,

The last time you saw me, I was a teenager. I was a high school student, and I had long hair. Now I'm 20 years old, and I'm a student at the university. I study computers. I play soccer every week. I really like it here, and I have a lot of friends. We usually go hiking on the weekend. I'm sending you a picture of me at my school. I have short hair now, and I usually wear jeans. In this picture, I'm wearing a dress. I hope you like the picture.

Please come and visit me.

Love,
Annie

1. How old is Annie? _She's 20 years old._____

2. What does she study? _____

3. When does she play soccer? _____

4. When does she go hiking? _____

5. What does she usually wear? _____

6. What is she wearing in the picture? _____

Unit 1 Personal information

Name: _____

Lesson E *Writing*

A Look at the pictures. Match the sentence parts.

1. Dan has   a. short curly hair.
2. Dan is wearing a   b. plaid shirt.
3. Dave has   c. short straight hair.
4. Dave is wearing a   d. striped shirt.

Dan   Dave

B Look at the schedule. Circle the answers.

	After class	On Thursday night	On the weekend
Dan	studies in the library	watches movies	fixes things in the house
Dave	goes to the supermarket	plays basketball	cooks dinner for his family

1. When does Dan fix things in the house?   a. after class   b. on the weekend
2. When does Dan watch movies?   a. on Thursday night   b. on the weekend
3. When does Dan study in the library?   a. on Thursday night   b. after class
4. When does Dave cook dinner for his family?   a. after class   b. on the weekend
5. When does Dave go to the supermarket?   a. on Thursday night   b. after class

C Complete the paragraph. Use some words more than once.

after class	curly	on the weekend	On Thursday night	straight

Dan and Dave are brothers. Dan has short _____*straight*_____

hair. Dave has short _____ hair.

_____ , Dan watches movies. He fixes things in

the house _____ . Dave goes to the supermarket

_____ . _____ , he plays

basketball.

Name: _____

Lesson E *Writing*

A Look at the pictures. Complete the sentences. Use some words more than once.

| curly | plaid | short | straight | striped |

1. Dan has _____*short*_____ _____*straight*_____ hair.

2. Dan is wearing a _____ shirt.

3. Dave has _____ _____ hair.

4. Dave is wearing a _____ shirt.

Dan   Dave

B Look at the schedule. Complete the sentences.

	After class	On Thursday night	On the weekend
Dan	studies in the library	watches movies	fixes things in the house
Dave	goes to the supermarket	plays basketball	cooks dinner for his family

1. Dan fixes things in the house *on the weekend* _____ .

2. Dan watches movies _____ .

3. Dan studies in the library _____ .

4. Dave cooks dinner for his family _____ .

5. Dave goes to the supermarket _____ .

C Complete the paragraph.

   Dan and Dave are brothers. Dan has short _____*straight*_____
hair. Dave has short _____ hair. On _____
_____ , Dan watches movies. He _____
things in the house on the weekend. Dave goes to the supermarket
_____ _____ . _____ Thursday
_____ , he plays basketball.

14   Add Ventures 2

© Cambridge University Press 2008 **Photocopiable**

Name: _____

Lesson E | Writing

A Look at the pictures. Complete the sentences.

1. Dan has _short straight hair_____ .
2. Dan is wearing _____ .
3. Dave has _____ .
4. Dave is wearing _____ .

Dan   Dave

B Look at the schedule. Answer the questions.

	After class	On Thursday night	On the weekend
Dan	studies in the library	watches movies	fixes things in the house
Dave	goes to the supermarket	plays basketball	cooks dinner for his family

1. When does Dan fix things in the house? _on the weekend_____
2. When does Dan watch movies? _____
3. When does Dan study in the library? _____
4. When does Dave cook dinner for his family? _____
5. When does Dave go to the supermarket? _____

C Complete the paragraph.

Dan and Dave are brothers. Dan has short ___straight___ hair. Dave

has _____ _____ hair. On _____ _____ ,

Dan watches movies. He _____ _____ in the house

on the _____ . Dave goes to the supermarket _____

_____ . _____ Thursday _____ , he plays

basketball.

Lesson F *Another view*

A Read the paragraph. Circle the answers.

> Susan ordered a large green sweater, three pairs of medium blue socks, one extra large green coat, and two pairs of red shoes in size 7. One sweater costs $39. Socks are $5 for each pair. One coat costs $57. Shoes are $25 for each pair.

1. How much is one sweater?   a. $39   b. $57
2. How much are three pairs of socks?   a. $5   b. $15
3. How much is one coat?   a. $39   b. $57
4. How much are two pairs of red shoes? a. $45   b. $50

B Use the information from Exercise A. Complete the order form. Write the total.

Order Form					
Item number	Quantity	Size	Color	Item name	Price
156B	1			sweater	$39
288C	3 pairs	medium	blue		
478A	1		green		$57
560F	2 pairs		red	shoes	
				Total	

C Read the paragraph. Complete a new order form. Write the total.

> Miki ordered a small purple sweater, five pairs of large black socks, one medium blue coat, and two pairs of brown shoes in size 9. One sweater is $48. Socks are $7 for each pair. One coat is $29. The shoes are $53 for each pair.

Order Form					
Item number	Quantity	Size	Color	Item name	Price
111B	1		purple		$48
452C	5 pairs	large	black		
344A	2 pairs		brown		$106
650F	1	medium		coat	
				Total	

Name: _____

Lesson F Another view

A Read the paragraph. Circle the answers.

> Susan ordered a large green sweater, three pairs of medium blue socks, one extra large green coat, and two pairs of red shoes in size 7. One sweater costs $39. Socks are $5 for each pair. One coat costs $57. Shoes are $25 for each pair.

1. How much is one sweater?   a. $25   (b. $39)   c. $57
2. How much are three pairs of socks?   a. $5   b. $15   c. $20
3. How much is one coat?   a. $25   b. $39   c. $57
4. How much are two pairs of red shoes?   a. $45   b. $50   c. $78

B Use the information from Exercise A. Complete the order form. Write the total.

Order Form					
Item number	*Quantity*	*Size*	*Color*	*Item name*	*Price*
156B	1				$39
288C	pairs	medium	blue		
478A			green		$57
560F	2 pairs			shoes	
				Total	

C Read the paragraph. Complete a new order form. Write the total.

> Miki ordered a small purple sweater, five pairs of large black socks, one medium blue coat, and two pairs of brown shoes in size 9. One sweater is $48. Socks are $7 for each pair. One coat is $29. The shoes are $53 for each pair.

Order Form					
Item number	*Quantity*	*Size*	*Color*	*Item name*	*Price*
111B	1		purple		
452C	pairs	large	black		
344A	2 pairs				$106
650F		medium		coat	
				Total	

Lesson F Another view

■ ■ ☑

A Read the paragraph. Answer the questions.

> Susan ordered a large green sweater, three pairs of medium blue socks, one extra large green coat, and two pairs of red shoes in size 7. One sweater costs $39. Socks are $5 for each pair. One coat costs $57. Shoes are $25 for each pair.

1. How much is one sweater? _$39_____

2. How much are three pairs of socks? _____

3. How much is one coat? _____

4. How much are two pairs of red shoes? _____

B Use the information from Exercise A. Complete the order form. Write the total.

Order Form					
Item number	Quantity	Size	Color	Item name	Price
156B					$39
288C	pairs	medium			
478A			green		
560F	2 pairs				
				Total	

C Read the paragraph. Complete a new order form. Write the total.

> Miki ordered a small purple sweater, five pairs of large black socks, one medium blue coat, and two pairs of brown shoes in size 9. One sweater is $48. Socks are $7 for each pair. One coat is $29. The shoes are $53 for each pair.

Order Form					
Item number	Quantity	Size	Color	Item name	Price
111B			purple		
452C			black		
344A	2 pairs				
650F		medium			
				Total	

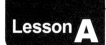

Unit 2 At school

Lesson A *Get ready*

Name: _____

A Look at the picture. Write the words.

computer lab	hall	keyboard	lab instructor	monitor	mouse

1. a c *omputer* l*ab*
2. a m_____

3. a m_____
4. a k_____

5. a l_____ i_____
6. a h_____

B Read the e-mail. Match the questions with the answers.

> **To: taki@cup.org**
> **From: miho@cup.org**
> **Subject: keyboarding class**
>
> Hi Taki,
>
>   How are you? I am in the computer lab at school. I really like keyboarding class. I think it is going to help me in college. Larry Smith is my lab instructor. You can register for this class next week.
>
> Best wishes,
> Miho

1. What class is Miho taking?   a. Miho's lab instructor

2. Where did Miho write the e-mail?   b. keyboarding class

3. Where does Miho think the class is going to help her?   c. in the computer lab

4. Who is Larry Smith?   d. in college

© Cambridge University Press 2008 **Photocopiable**   **Add Ventures 2**   **19**

Name: _____

Lesson A *Get ready*

A Look at the picture. Write the words.

| a computer lab | a hall | a keyboard | a lab instructor | a monitor | a mouse |

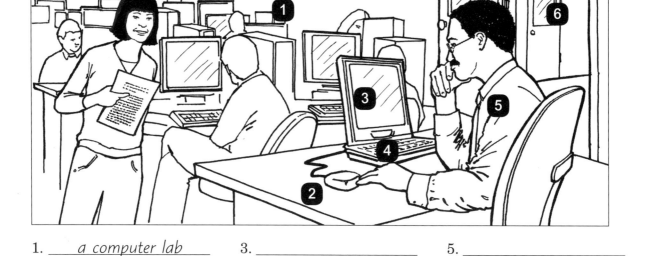

1. _____a computer lab_____   3. _____   5. _____

2. _____   4. _____   6. _____

B Read the e-mail. Complete the sentences.

> **To: taki@cup.org**
> **From: miho@cup.org**
> **Subject: keyboarding class**
>
> Hi Taki,
>
>   How are you? I am in the computer lab at school. I really like keyboarding class. I think it is going to help me in college. Larry Smith is my lab instructor. You can register for this class next week.
>
> Best wishes,
> Miho

1. Miho is taking a _keyboarding class_ .

2. Miho wrote the e-mail in the _____ .

3. Miho thinks the class is going to help her _____ .

4. Larry Smith is _____ .

Lesson A **Get ready**

Name: _____

A Look at the picture. Write the words.

1. _a computer lab_   3. _____   5. _____

2. _____   4. _____   6. _____

B Read the e-mail. Answer the questions. Write complete sentences.

> **To: taki@cup.org**
> **From: miho@cup.org**
> **Subject: keyboarding class**
>
> Hi Taki,
>
> How are you? I am in the computer lab at school. I really like keyboarding class. I think it is going to help me in college. Larry Smith is my lab instructor. You can register for this class next week.
>
> Best wishes,
> Miho

1. What class is Miho taking? _Miho is taking a keyboarding class._

2. Where did Miho write the e-mail? _____

_____

3. Where does Miho think the class is going to help her? _____

_____

4. Who is Larry Smith? _____

_____

Name:

Lesson B *What do you want to do?*

A Match the questions with the answers.

1. What do you want to do?
2. What does he want to do?
3. What do they need to do?
4. What does she need to do?

a. They need to study auto mechanics.
b. She needs to go to college.
c. I want to get a job.
d. He wants to become a citizen.

B Circle the answers.

1. Ron wants to get a driver's license. What does he need to do?
   He **need to / needs to** take driving lessons.

2. You want to become a citizen. What do you need to do?
   I **need to / needs to** take a citizenship class.

3. They want to learn computer skills. What do they need to do?
   They **need to / needs to** take a computer class.

4. He wants to make more money. What does he need to do?
   He **need to / needs to** get a second job.

5. Pam wants to get her GED. What does she need to do?
   She **need to / needs to** take a GED class.

C Match the sentences with the advice.

1. I want to work in a restaurant.
2. I want to get a driver's license.
3. I want to become a citizen.
4. I want to go to college.
5. I want to fix cars.

a. Why don't you take driving lessons?
b. You could take a citizenship class.
c. Why don't you study auto mechanics?
d. You could take a cooking class.
e. Why don't you talk to a counselor?

D Answer the questions. Use your own information.

1. What do you want to do?

   I want to _____ .

2. What do you need to do?

   I need to _____ .

Name: _____

Lesson B *What do you want to do?*

A Read the questions. Complete the answers.

1. What do you want to do?   I ___*want to*___ get a job.

2. What does he want to do?   He _____ become a citizen.

3. What do they need to do?   They _____ study auto mechanics.

4. What does she need to do?   She _____ go to college.

B Answer the questions.

get a second job	take a computer class	take a GED class
take a citizenship class	take driving lessons	

1. Ron wants to get a driver's license. What does he need to do?

   He needs to take driving lessons. _____

2. You want to become a citizen. What do you need to do?

   _____

3. They want to learn computer skills. What do they need to do?

   _____

4. He wants to make more money. What does he need to do?

   _____

5. Pam wants to get her GED. What does she need to do?

   _____

C Give advice. Complete the sentences.

1. I want to work in a restaurant.   You ___*could*___ take a cooking class.

2. I want to get a driver's license.   Why _____ take driving lessons?

3. I want to become a citizen.   You _____ take a citizenship class.

4. I want to go to college.   Why _____ talk to a counselor?

5. I want to fix cars.   Why _____ study auto mechanics?

D Answer the questions. Use your own information.

1. What do you want to do?

   _____

2. What do you need to do?

   _____

Name: _____

Lesson B *What do you want to do?*

A Read the answers. Write questions.

1. *What do you want to do* _____ ? I want to get a job.
2. _____ ? He wants to become a citizen.
3. _____ ? They need to study auto mechanics.
4. _____ ? She needs to go to college.

B Answer the questions.

1. Ron wants to get a driver's license. What does he need to do?
   He needs to take driving lessons. _____

2. You want to become a citizen. What do you need to do?
   _____

3. They want to learn computer skills. What do they need to do?
   _____

4. He wants to make more money. What does he need to do?
   _____

5. Pam wants to get her GED. What does she need to do?
   _____

C Give advice. Complete the sentences.

1. I want to work in a restaurant.   You could *take a cooking class* .
2. I want to get a driver's license.   Why don't you _____ ?
3. I want to become a citizen.   You could _____ .
4. I want to go to college.   Why don't you _____ ?
5. I want to fix cars.   Why don't you _____ ?

D Write sentences about what you want to do and what you need to do.

_____

_____

_____

Name: _____

Lesson C *What will you do?*

A Look at the pictures. Match the questions with the answers.

| Sue | Damian | Asha | Carlos |

1. What will Sue do in the next five years?
2. What will Damian do next year?
3. What will Asha do next fall?
4. What will Carlos do in the next two years?

a. She will probably go to college.
b. Maybe she will buy a house.
c. He will most likely learn a new language.
d. He will probably open a business.

B Look at Pat's schedule. Complete the sentences. Use *will* or *won't*.

Monday	Tuesday	Wednesday
morning: work	*morning: work*	*morning: do homework*
afternoon: English class	*afternoon: English class*	*afternoon: English class*

1. Pat ____*won't*____ do homework on Tuesday morning.
2. She _____ work on Tuesday morning.
3. She _____ go to English class on Monday afternoon.
4. She _____ work on Wednesday morning.
5. She _____ go to English class on Monday morning.

Name: _____

Lesson C *What will you do?*

A Look at the pictures. Complete the sentences.

| Sue | Damian | Asha | Carlos |

| buy a house | go to college | learn a new language | open a business |

1. What will Sue do in the next five years?   Maybe she will _buy a house_____ .
2. What will Damian do next year?   He will most likely _____ .
3. What will Asha do next fall?   She will probably _____ .
4. What will Carlos do in the next two years?   He will probably _____ .

B Look at Pat's schedule. Complete the sentences. Use *will* or *won't*.

Monday	Tuesday	Wednesday
morning: work	morning: work	morning: do homework
afternoon: English class	afternoon: English class	afternoon: English class

1. Pat ____won't do homework____ on Tuesday morning.
      (do homework)

2. She _____ on Tuesday morning.
         (work)

3. She _____ on Monday afternoon.
      (go to English class)

4. She _____ on Wednesday morning.
            (work)

5. She _____ on Monday morning.
      (go to English class)

Name: _____

Lesson C *What will you do?* ■ ■ ☑

A Look at the pictures. Complete the sentences.

| Sue | Damian | Asha | Carlos |

1. What will Sue do in the next five years?   Maybe she will *buy a house* _____ .
2. What will Damian do next year?   He will most likely _____ .
3. What will Asha do next fall?   She will probably _____ .
4. What will Carlos do in the next two years?   He will probably _____ .

B Look at Pat's schedule. Write sentences. Use *will* or *won't*.

Monday	Tuesday	Wednesday
morning: work	morning: work	morning: do homework
afternoon: English class	afternoon: English class	afternoon: English class

1. *Pat won't do homework on Tuesday morning.* _____
   (do homework / Tuesday morning)
2. _____
   (work / Tuesday morning)
3. _____
   (go to English class / Monday afternoon)
4. _____
   (work / Wednesday morning)
5. _____
   (go to English class / Monday morning)

Name: _____

Lesson D *Reading*

A Match the pictures with the words.

a. nursing   b. accounting   c. culinary arts   d. landscape design

B Read about Bettina's goal. Circle the answers.

> I want to open my own hotel. I need to take three steps to reach my goal. First, I need to speak and write more English. Second, I need to study hotel management. Third, I need to work in a hotel for three or four years. I will probably open my hotel in five or six years.

1. Bettina's goal is to   a. take a business class.   (b. open a hotel.)

2. Bettina has to take   a. five steps.   b. three steps.

3. The second step is to   a. study hotel management.   b. write more English.

4. The third step is to   a. study hotel management.   b. work in a hotel.

5. She wants to reach her goal in   a. three or four years.   b. five or six years.

C Answer the questions. Use your own information.

1. What vocational course do you want or need to take?

_____

2. Why do you want or need to take this course?

_____

Lesson D Reading

A Look at the pictures. Write the vocational courses.

| accounting | culinary arts | landscape design | nursing |

1. _culinary arts_
2. _____
3. _____
4. _____

B Read about Bettina's goal. Complete the sentences.

> *I want to open my own hotel. I need to take three steps to reach my goal. First, I need to speak and write more English. Second, I need to study hotel management. Third, I need to work in a hotel for three or four years. I will probably open my hotel in five or six years.*

1. Bettina's goal is to _open a hotel_   .

2. Bettina has to take _____ .

3. The second step is to _____ .

4. The third step is to _____ .

5. She wants to reach her goal in _____ .

C Answer the questions. Use your own information.

1. What vocational course do you want or need to take?

   _____

2. Why do you want or need to take this course?

   _____

3. Where do you want to take this course?

   _____

Lesson D *Reading*

A Look at the pictures. Write the vocational courses.

__culinary arts__   _____   _____   _____

B Read about Bettina's goal. Answer the questions.

> *I want to open my own hotel. I need to take three steps to reach my goal. First, I need to speak and write more English. Second, I need to study hotel management. Third, I need to work in a hotel for three or four years. I will probably open my hotel in five or six years.*

1. What is Bettina's goal? _Bettina's goal is to open a hotel._

2. How many steps does Bettina have to take? _____

3. What is her second step? _____

4. What is her third step? _____

5. When does Bettina want to reach her goal? _____

C Answer the questions. Use your own information.

1. What vocational course do you want or need to take?

   _____

2. Why do you want or need to take this course?

   _____

3. Where do you want to take this course?

   _____

4. How will the course help you to reach your goals?

   _____

Lesson E *Writing*

Name: _____

A Read about Shen's goal. Complete the chart.

> ## My Goal
>
> I love to cook, and my goal is to own a restaurant. I need to take three steps to reach my goal. First, I need to study culinary arts. Second, I need to work as a cook in three or four different restaurants. Third, I need to take business classes. I want to reach my goal in ten years.

Shen's goal:	He needs to:	He wants to reach his goal in:
His goal is to own a restaurant.	1. _____ 2. _____ 3. _____	*ten years*

B Number the sentences in the correct order.

__1__ My name is Karen.

____ Second, I need to talk to nurses to learn more about what they do.

__2__ My goal is to go to nursing school.

____ Third, I need to talk to a counselor about nursing schools.

____ Maybe I'll be ready to start nursing school next year.

____ First, I need to speak, read, and write English better.

__3__ There are three steps I need to take to reach my goal.

C Answer the questions. Use the information from Exercise B.

to go to nursing school	to speak, read, and write English better
to talk to a counselor	to talk to nurses

1. What is Karen's goal? *Karen's goal is to go to nursing school.* _____

2. First, what does she need to do? _____

3. Second, what does she need to do? _____

4. Third, what does she need to do? _____

Lesson **E** *Writing*

Name: _____

A Read about Shen's goal. Complete the chart.

> # My Goal
>
> I love to cook, and my goal is to own a restaurant. I need to take three steps to reach my goal. First, I need to study culinary arts. Second, I need to work as a cook in three or four different restaurants. Third, I need to take business classes. I want to reach my goal in ten years.

Shen's goal:	He needs to:	He wants to reach his goal in:
	1. _____	*ten years*
	2. _____	
	3. _____	

B Number the sentences in the correct order.

_1_ My name is Karen.

___ Second, I need to talk to nurses to learn more about what they do.

_2_ My goal is to go to nursing school.

___ Third, I need to talk to a counselor about nursing schools.

___ Maybe I'll be ready to start nursing school next year.

___ First, I need to speak, read, and write English better.

___ There are three steps I need to take to reach my goal.

C Answer the questions. Use the information from Exercise B.

1. What is Karen's goal? *Karen's goal is to go to nursing school.* _____

2. First, what does she need to do? _____

3. Second, what does she need to do? _____

4. Third, what does she need to do? _____

Lesson E *Writing*

A Read about Shen's goal. Complete the chart.

My Goal

I love to cook, and my goal is to own a restaurant. I need to take three steps to reach my goal. First, I need to study culinary arts. Second, I need to work as a cook in three or four different restaurants. Third, I need to take business classes. I want to reach my goal in ten years.

Shen's goal:	He needs to:	He wants to reach his goal in:
	1. _____ 2. _____ 3. _____	

B Number the sentences in the correct order.

__1__ My name is Karen.

_____ Second, I need to talk to nurses to learn more about what they do.

_____ My goal is to go to nursing school.

_____ Third, I need to talk to a counselor about nursing schools.

_____ Maybe I'll be ready to start nursing school next year.

_____ First, I need to speak, read, and write English better.

_____ There are three steps I need to take to reach my goal.

C Answer the questions. Use the information from Exercise B.

1. What is Karen's goal? *Karen's goal is to go to nursing school.* _____

2. First, what does she need to do? _____

3. Second, what does she need to do? _____

4. Third, what does she need to do? _____

5. When does she want to reach her goal? _____

Lesson F *Another view*

A Look at the course catalog. Circle the answers.

COURSE CATALOG

ACCOUNTING FOR BEGINNERS *Learn how to become an accountant.* Fee: $98 Days: Saturdays and Sundays Time: 8:00–11:00 a.m. Instructor: Meena Roy	**NURSING FOR BEGINNERS** *Learn about the steps you need to take to become a nurse.* Fee: $85 Days: Fridays Time: 7:00–9:00 p.m. Instructor: Raphael Rivera
INTRODUCTION TO LANDSCAPE DESIGN *Learn about plants and how to take care of them.* Fee: $100 Days: Tuesdays and Thursdays Time: 7:00–8:30 p.m. Instructor: Lee Chung	**HOME REPAIRS** *Learn how to fix your home and save money on home repairs.* Fee: $75 Days: Mondays and Wednesdays Time: 6:30–8:30 p.m. Instructor: Javier Espinoza

1. How much is the nursing class?
   a. $75
   b. $85   *(circled)*
   c. $98

2. When is the landscape design class?
   a. Monday and Wednesday
   b. Saturday and Sunday
   c. Tuesday and Thursday

3. What time is the home repairs class?
   a. 8:00–11:00 a.m.
   b. 6:30–8:30 p.m.
   c. 7:00–9:00 p.m.

4. Who teaches the accounting class?
   a. Lee Chung
   b. Meena Roy
   c. Raphael Rivera

B Look at the schedule. Circle *T* (true) or *F* (false).

English Writing Class Schedule				
Section	Time	Days	Room	Instructor
01	8:00–8:50 a.m.	Mon., Wed., Fri.	117	Mr. Davis
02	9:00–9:50 a.m.	Mon., Wed., Fri.	117	Mr. Davis
03	11:00 a.m.–12:15 p.m.	Tues., Thurs.	221	Ms. Williams
04	7:00–7:50 p.m.	Mon., Wed., Fri.	117	Ms. Porter

1. The 8:00 a.m. class meets on Monday and Wednesday only.   T / **F** *(F circled)*

2. Section 03 meets in Room 221.   T / F

3. Ms. Williams does not teach on Tuesday and Thursday.   T / F

4. Ms. Porter teaches Section 02.   T / F

Lesson **F** *Another view*

A Look at the course catalog. Circle the answers.

COURSE CATALOG

ACCOUNTING FOR BEGINNERS *Learn how to become an accountant.* Fee: $98 Days: Saturdays and Sundays Time: 8:00–11:00 a.m. Instructor: Meena Roy	**NURSING FOR BEGINNERS** *Learn about the steps you need to take to become a nurse.* Fee: $85 Days: Fridays Time: 7:00–9:00 p.m. Instructor: Raphael Rivera
INTRODUCTION TO LANDSCAPE DESIGN *Learn about plants and how to take care of them.* Fee: $100 Days: Tuesdays and Thursdays Time: 7:00–8:30 p.m. Instructor: Lee Chung	**HOME REPAIRS** *Learn how to fix your home and save money on home repairs.* Fee: $75 Days: Mondays and Wednesdays Time: 6:30–8:30 p.m. Instructor: Javier Espinoza

1. How much is the nursing class?
   a. $75   c. $98
   (b. $85)   d. $100

2. When is the landscape design class?
   a. Monday and Wednesday
   b. Saturday and Sunday
   c. Tuesday and Thursday
   d. Friday

3. What time is the home repairs class?
   a. 8:00–11:00 a.m.   c. 7:00–8:30 p.m.
   b. 6:30–8:30 p.m.   d. 7:00–9:00 p.m.

4. Who teaches the accounting class?
   a. Javier Espinoza
   b. Lee Chung
   c. Meena Roy
   d. Raphael Rivera

B Look at the schedule. Complete the sentences.

Section	Time	Days	Room	Instructor
English Writing Class Schedule				
01	8:00–8:50 a.m.	Mon., Wed., Fri.	117	Mr. Davis
02	9:00–9:50 a.m.	Mon., Wed., Fri.	117	Mr. Davis
03	11:00 a.m.–12:15 p.m.	Tues., Thurs.	221	Ms. Williams
04	7:00–7:50 p.m.	Mon., Wed., Fri.	117	Ms. Porter

1. The 8:00 a.m. class meets on *Monday, Wednesday, and Friday* .

2. Section 03 meets in Room _____ .

3. Ms. Williams does not teach on _____ .

4. Ms. Porter teaches Section _____ .

Name: _____

Lesson F *Another view*

A Look at the course catalog. Write the answers.

COURSE CATALOG

ACCOUNTING FOR BEGINNERS
Learn how to become an accountant.

Fee: $98
Days: Saturdays and Sundays
Time: 8:00–11:00 a.m.
Instructor: Meena Roy

NURSING FOR BEGINNERS
Learn about the steps you need to take to become a nurse.

Fee: $85
Days: Fridays
Time: 7:00–9:00 p.m.
Instructor: Raphael Rivera

INTRODUCTION TO LANDSCAPE DESIGN
Learn about plants and how to take care of them.

Fee: $100
Days: Tuesdays and Thursdays
Time: 7:00–8:30 p.m.
Instructor: Lee Chung

HOME REPAIRS
Learn how to fix your home and save money on home repairs.

Fee: $75
Days: Mondays and Wednesdays
Time: 6:30–8:30 p.m.
Instructor: Javier Espinoza

1. How much is the nursing class? *$85* _____

2. When is the landscape design class? _____

3. What time is the home repairs class? _____

4. Who teaches the accounting class? _____

B Look at the schedule. Answer the questions.

Section	Time	Days	Room	Instructor
English Writing Class Schedule				
01	8:00–8:50 a.m.	Mon., Wed., Fri.	117	Mr. Davis
02	9:00–9:50 a.m.	Mon., Wed., Fri.	117	Mr. Davis
03	11:00 a.m.–12:15 p.m.	Tues., Thurs.	221	Ms. Williams
04	7:00–7:50 p.m.	Mon., Wed., Fri.	117	Ms. Porter

1. When does the 8:00 a.m. class meet? *on Monday, Wednesday, and Friday* _____

2. Where does Section 03 meet? _____

3. Ms. Williams doesn't teach on which days? _____

4. Which section does Ms. Porter teach? _____

Name: _____

Lesson **A** *Get ready*

A Match the pictures with the words.

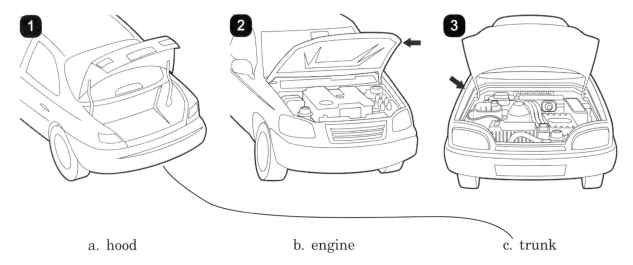

a. hood   b. engine   c. trunk

B Complete the sentences.

1. Marta _____*picked up*_____ her children.
   (bought / picked up)

2. She _____ to the supermarket.
   (broke / went)

3. She _____ some groceries.
   (bought / called)

4. Her car _____ down.
   (bought / broke)

5. She _____ her mother for help.
   (called / went)

C Complete the sentences. Use your own information.

1. Yesterday, I bought _____ .

2. Yesterday, I called _____ .

3. Yesterday, I went _____ .

Name: _____

Lesson A Get ready

A Look at the pictures. Write the words.

engine	hood	trunk

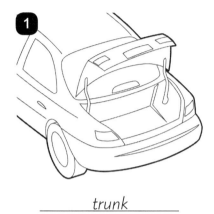
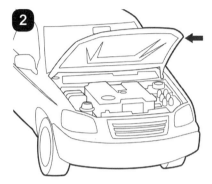
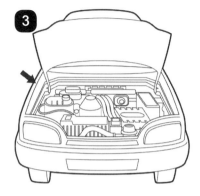

1

2

3

_____*trunk*_____   _____   _____

B Complete the sentences.

bought	broke	called	picked up	went

1. Marta _____*picked up*_____ her children.

2. She _____ to the supermarket.

3. She _____ some groceries.

4. Her car _____ down.

5. She _____ her mother for help.

C Complete the sentences. Use your own information.

1. Yesterday, I bought _____ .

2. Yesterday, I called _____ .

3. Yesterday, I went _____ .

4. Yesterday, I picked up _____ .

Name: _____

Lesson A *Get ready*

A Look at the pictures. Write the words.

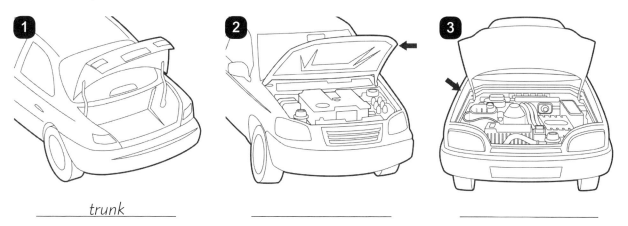

_____trunk_____   _____   _____

B Complete the sentences. Use the past tense.

break	buy	call	go	pick up

1. Marta _____*picked up*_____ her children.

2. She _____ to the supermarket.

3. She _____ some groceries.

4. Her car _____ down.

5. She _____ her mother for help.

C Complete the sentences. Use your own information.

1. Yesterday, I bought _____ .

2. Yesterday, I called _____ .

3. Yesterday, I went _____ .

4. Yesterday, I picked up _____ .

5. When I have a car problem, _____ .

Lesson B *What did you do last weekend?*

A Write the past tense.

1. stay _s_ _t_ _a_ _y_ _e_ _d_   5. drive __ __ __ __ __

2. buy __ __ __ __ __ __ __   6. take __ __ __ __ __

3. eat __ __ __   7. fix __ __ __ __ __

4. meet __ __ __   8. barbecue __ __ __ __ __ __ __ __ __

B Look at Julie's schedule. Answer the questions.

Sunday	Monday	Tuesday	Wednesday	Thursday	Friday	Saturday
stay home	have a picnic	buy groceries	read a book	meet a friend	go to the movies	play soccer

bought	met	played	read

1. What did Julie do on Wednesday?   She _____*read*_____ a book.

2. What did Julie do on Tuesday?   She _____ groceries.

3. What did Julie do on Thursday?   She _____ a friend.

4. What did Julie do on Saturday?   She _____ soccer.

C Look at Julie's schedule in Exercise B. Circle the answers.

1. **A** Did Julie stay home last Sunday?

   B (Yes, she did.)/ No, she didn't.

2. **A** Did Julie buy groceries last Monday?

   B Yes, she did. / No, she didn't.

3. **A** Did Julie meet a friend last Friday?

   B Yes, she did. / No, she didn't.

4. **A** Did Julie play soccer last Saturday?

   B Yes, she did. / No, she didn't.

D Answer the questions. Use your own information.

1. What did you do last night? _____

2. What did you do last Saturday? _____

Lesson B *What did you do last weekend?* ■ ☑ ■

A Write the past tense.

1. stay ____stayed____   6. take _____

2. buy _____   7. fix _____

3. eat _____   8. barbecue _____

4. meet _____   9. go _____

5. drive _____   10. read _____

B Look at Julie's schedule. Answer the questions. Use the past tense.

Sunday	Monday	Tuesday	Wednesday	Thursday	Friday	Saturday
stay home	have a picnic	buy groceries	read a book	meet a friend	go to the movies	play soccer

1. What did Julie do on Wednesday?   She _____read_____ a book.

2. What did Julie do on Tuesday?   She _____ groceries.

3. What did Julie do on Thursday?   She _____ a friend.

4. What did Julie do on Saturday?   She _____ soccer.

C Look at Julie's schedule in Exercise B. Complete the conversations.

1. **A** Did Julie stay home last Sunday?

   B ___Yes___ , ___she did___ .

2. **A** Did Julie buy groceries last Monday?

   B _____ , _____ .

3. **A** Did Julie meet a friend last Friday?

   B _____ , _____ .

4. **A** Did Julie play soccer last Saturday?

   B _____ , _____ .

D Answer the questions. Use your own information.

1. What did you do last night? _____

2. What did you do last Saturday? _____

3. Did you eat in a restaurant last weekend? _____

Lesson B *What did you do last weekend?*

A Write the past tense.

1. stay ___stayed___   7. fix _____

2. buy _____   8. barbecue _____

3. eat _____   9. go _____

4. meet _____   10. read _____

5. drive _____   11. study _____

6. take _____   12. play _____

B Look at Julie's schedule. Answer the questions. Use the past tense.

Sunday	Monday	Tuesday	Wednesday	Thursday	Friday	Saturday
stay home	have a picnic	buy groceries	read a book	meet a friend	go to the movies	play soccer

1. What did Julie do on Wednesday?   *She read a book.* _____

2. What did Julie do on Tuesday?   _____

3. What did Julie do on Thursday?   _____

4. What did Julie do on Saturday?   _____

C Look at Julie's schedule in Exercise B. Complete the conversations.

1. **A** *Did Julie stay home last Sunday* _____ ? (stay home)

   B Yes, she did.

2. **A** _____ ? (buy groceries)

   B No, she didn't. She had a picnic.

3. **A** _____ ? (meet a friend)

   B No, she didn't. She went to the movies.

4. **A** _____ ? (play soccer)

   B Yes, she did.

D Answer the questions. Use your own information.

1. What did you do last night? _____

2. What did you do last Saturday? _____

3. Did you eat in a restaurant last weekend? _____

4. Did you read a book this week? _____

Name: _____

Lesson C *When do you usually play soccer?*

A Look at the chart. Circle the answers.

	usually	yesterday
Angel	eats dinner at 6:00 p.m.	ate dinner at 7:30 p.m.
Suki	goes to the gym before work	went to the gym after work
Arturo and Bonita	study at night	studied in the morning

1. When does Angel usually eat dinner? (a. at 6:00 p.m.) b. at 7:30 p.m.

2. When did Angel eat dinner yesterday? a. at 6:00 p.m. b. at 7:30 p.m.

3. When does Suki usually go to the gym? a. after work b. before work

4. When did Suki go to the gym yesterday? a. after work b. before work

5. When do Arturo and Bonita usually study? a. at night b. in the morning

6. When did Arturo and Bonita study yesterday? a. at night b. in the morning

B Circle the answers.

1. **A** When **did** / **does** Tara usually play soccer?

   B She usually **played** / **plays** soccer on the weekend.

2. **A** When **did** / **does** Jack eat dinner last night?

   B He **ate** / **eats** dinner at 7:30 p.m.

3. **A** When **did** / **does** Janet go shopping yesterday?

   B She **goes** / **went** shopping after work.

C Answer the questions. Use your own information.

1. What time do you usually eat dinner? _____

2. What time did you eat dinner yesterday? _____

Lesson C *When do you usually play soccer?*

A Look at the chart. Answer the questions.

	usually	yesterday
Angel	eats dinner at 6:00 p.m.	ate dinner at 7:30 p.m.
Suki	goes to the gym before work	went to the gym after work
Arturo and Bonita	study at night	studied in the morning

1. When does Angel usually eat dinner? *at 6:00 p.m.* _____

2. When did Angel eat dinner yesterday? _____

3. When does Suki usually go to the gym? _____

4. When did Suki go to the gym yesterday? _____

5. When do Arturo and Bonita usually study? _____

6. When did Arturo and Bonita study yesterday? _____

B Complete the conversations. Use the simple present or the simple past.

1. **A** When _____*does*_____ Tara usually play soccer?

   B She usually _____ soccer on the weekend.

2. **A** When _____ Jack eat dinner last night?

   B He _____ dinner at 7:30 p.m.

3. **A** When _____ Janet go shopping yesterday?

   B She _____ shopping after work.

C Complete the questions with *do* or *did*. Answer the questions.
Use your own information.

1. What time _____ you usually eat dinner? _____

2. What time _____ you eat dinner yesterday? _____

Lesson C — *When do you usually play soccer?* ■ ■

A Look at the chart. Read the answers. Complete the questions.

	usually	yesterday
Angel	eats dinner at 6:00 p.m.	ate dinner at 7:30 p.m.
Suki	goes to the gym before work	went to the gym after work
Arturo and Bonita	study at night	studied in the morning

1. When __*does*__ Angel usually _____*eat*_____ dinner? at 6:00 p.m.

2. When _____ Angel _____ dinner yesterday? at 7:30 p.m.

3. When _____ Suki usually _____ to the gym? before work

4. When _____ Suki _____ to the gym yesterday? after work

5. When _____ Arturo and Bonita usually _____ ? at night

6. When _____ Arturo and Bonita _____ yesterday? in the morning

B Complete the conversations. Use the simple present or the simple past.

1. **A** When _____*does*_____ Tara usually play soccer?

   B She usually _____ soccer on the weekend.

2. **A** When _____ Jack eat dinner last night?

   B He _____ dinner at 7:30 p.m.

3. **A** When _____ Janet go shopping yesterday?

   B She _____ shopping after work.

4. **A** When _____ Marcos usually go to work?

   B He usually _____ to work at 8:00 a.m.

C Complete the questions with *do* or *did*. Answer the questions.
Use your own information.

1. What time _____ you usually eat dinner? _____

2. What time _____ you eat dinner yesterday? _____

3. When _____ you usually study? _____

4. When _____ you study yesterday? _____

Lesson D **Reading** ☑ ■ ■

A Match the pictures with the words.

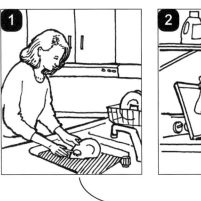  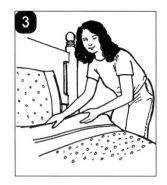 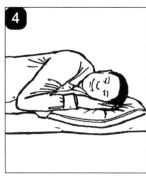

a. make the bed   b. take a nap   c. do the dishes   d. do the laundry

B Read Marie's journal. Circle the answers.

> *What a day! On Thursday night, I usually cook dinner for my parents. I left work early and went to the supermarket. I bought groceries. Then, I went home. First, I cleaned the house. Next, I cooked the food. I watched TV and waited for my parents. At 6:30 p.m., they weren't here. I called them, and they told me today is Wednesday. I made dinner on the wrong day!*

1. What does Marie usually do on Thursday night?   (She cooks dinner.)   She watches TV.

2. What did she do first at home?   She cleaned.   She cooked.

3. What did she do next?   She cooked.   She watched TV.

4. What did she do at 6:30?   She watched TV.   She called her parents.

C Number the sentences in the correct order.

_____ She bought groceries.

_____ She went home.

_____ She went to the supermarket.

_1_ Marie left work early.

Lesson D *Reading*   ■ ✓ ■

A Look at the pictures. Write the words.

| take a nap | do the dishes | make the bed | do the laundry |

  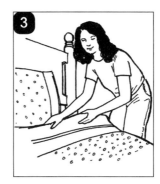 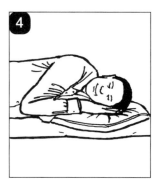

___do the dishes___   _____   _____   _____

B Read Marie's journal. Answer the questions.

> What a day! On Thursday night, I usually cook dinner for my parents. I left work early and went to the supermarket. I bought groceries. Then, I went home. First, I cleaned the house. Next, I cooked the food. I watched TV and waited for my parents. At 6:30 p.m., they weren't here. I called them, and they told me today is Wednesday. I made dinner on the wrong day!

1. What does Marie usually do on Thursday night? _She cooks dinner for her parents._

2. What did she do first at home? _____

3. What did she do next? _____

4. What did she do at 6:30? _____

C Number the sentences in the correct order.

_____ She bought groceries.

_____ She cleaned the house.

_____ She went home.

_____ She went to the supermarket.

_____ She watched TV.

_1_ Marie left work early.

_____ She cooked dinner.

Lesson D Reading

A Look at the pictures. Write the words.

   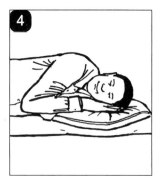

do the dishes _____ _____ _____ _____

B Read Marie's journal and the answers. Write questions.

> What a day! On Thursday night, I usually cook dinner for my parents. I left work early and went to the supermarket. I bought groceries. Then, I went home. First, I cleaned the house. Next, I cooked the food. I watched TV and waited for my parents. At 6:30 p.m., they weren't here. I called them, and they told me today is Wednesday. I made dinner on the wrong day!

1. What _does Marie usually do on Thursday night_ ? She cooks dinner for her parents.

2. What _____ ? First, she cleaned the house.

3. What _____ ? Next, she cooked.

4. What _____ ? She called her parents.

C Number the sentences in the correct order.

____ She bought groceries.

____ She called her parents.

____ She cleaned the house.

____ She went home.

____ She went to the supermarket.

____ She watched TV.

_1_ Marie left work early.

____ She waited for her parents.

____ She cooked dinner.

Lesson **E** *Writing*

Name: _____

A Look at the pictures. Complete the paragraph.

Min's Big Day

| ate | called | cleaned | listened | went |

My name is Min. Yesterday, I had a big party at my house. First, I _____*called*_____ my friends to tell them about the party. Next, I _____ shopping for food. At the party, we _____ to music and _____ good food. We had fun. Finally, I _____ the apartment. Now, I'm tired!

B Kay left a note for her husband. Number the sentences in the correct order.

_1_ Hi Eric,

____ Next, make some rice.

____ Thank you! I will be home at 7:15 p.m.

____ Finally, cut the vegetables.

_2_ I will be home late. Could you please make dinner?

____ First, cook the chicken.

____ See you soon!

C What did you do today?

First, I _____ .

Next, I _____ .

Finally, I _____ .

Name: _____

Lesson E *Writing*

A Look at the pictures. Complete the paragraph.

Min's Big Day

ate	cleaned	First	Next
called	Finally	listened	went

My name is Min. Yesterday, I had a big party at my house.

_____*First*_____ , I _____ my friends to tell them about the

party. _____ , I _____ shopping for food. At the

party, we _____ to music and _____ good food.

We had fun. _____ , I _____ the apartment. Now,

I'm tired!

B Kay left a note for her husband. Number the sentences in the correct order.

_1_ Hi Eric,

____ Next, make some rice.

____ Thank you! I will be home at 7:15 p.m.

____ Finally, cut the vegetables.

____ I will be home late. Could you please make dinner?

____ First, cook the chicken.

____ See you soon!

C Write three sentences about what you did today. Use *First*, *Next*, and *Finally*.

_____

_____

_____

Lesson **E** *Writing*

A Look at the pictures. Complete the paragraph.

ate	cleaned	First	listened	went
called	Finally	had	Next	Yesterday

> My name is Min. _____*Yesterday*_____ , I _____ a big party
> at my house. _____ , I _____ my friends to
> tell them about the party. _____ , I _____
> shopping for food. At the party, we _____ to music and
> _____ good food. We had fun. _____ , I
> _____ the apartment. Now, I'm tired!

B Kay left a note for her husband. Number the sentences in the correct order. Add commas.

__*1*__ Hi Eric

_____ Next make some rice.

_____ Thank you! I will be home at 7:15 p.m.

_____ Finally cut the vegetables.

_____ I will be home late. Could you please make dinner?

_____ First cook the chicken.

_____ See you soon!

C Write four sentences about what you did today. Use *First*, *Next*, *Finally*, and *In the end*.

_____

_____

_____

_____

Lesson F Another view

A Look at the cell phone calling plans. Circle the answers.

Phone Calling Plans			
Name	Cost	Monthly minutes	Additional minutes
Plan A	$24 a month	100	$0.10
Plan B	$58 a month	300	$0.25
Plan C	$69 a month	600	$0.32

1. How much is Plan A every month?   ($24) $58

2. How much is Plan C every month? $58 $69

3. How many monthly minutes does Plan B have?   300   600

4. How many monthly minutes does Plan C have?   300   600

5. How much is one additional minute with Plan A? $0.10 $0.25

B Look at the phone bill. Match the questions with the answers.

TALK TIME Phone Bill

Samir Patel   Phone number: (323) 555-0989
4555 Washington St.   Account number: 8099-0989
Los Angeles, CA 90040   Billing date: January 15, 2008

	Monthly minutes	Calling charges
Monthly plan – Plan B	300	$58
Additional minutes	20	$5
Total	320	$63

1. How many minutes come with Samir's plan?   a. 320 minutes

2. How many minutes did Samir use this month?   b. $58

3. How much is Samir's basic plan?   c. $5

4. How much did Samir pay for additional minutes? d. 300 minutes

C Check (✓) the answers. Use your own information.

1. When do you usually talk on the phone?   ___ morning   ___ afternoon   ___ night

2. How long do you usually talk on the phone? ___ 10–20 min. ___ 20–30 min. ___ 30+ min.

Lesson F *Another view*

A Look at the cell phone calling plans. Circle the answers.

Phone Calling Plans			
Name	*Cost*	*Monthly minutes*	*Additional minutes*
Plan A	$24 a month	100	$0.10
Plan B	$58 a month	300	$0.25
Plan C	$69 a month	600	$0.32

1. How much is Plan A every month? ($24) $58 $69
2. How much is Plan C every month? $24 $58 $69
3. How many monthly minutes does Plan B have? 100 300 600
4. How many monthly minutes does Plan C have? 100 300 600
5. How much is one additional minute with Plan A? $0.10 $0.25 $0.32

B Look at the phone bill. Answer the questions.

TALK TIME Phone Bill

Samir Patel
4555 Washington St.
Los Angeles, CA 90040

Phone number: (323) 555-0989
Account number: 8099-0989
Billing date: January 15, 2008

	Monthly minutes	Calling charges
Monthly plan – Plan B	300	$58
Additional minutes	20	$5
Total	320	$63

1. How many minutes come with Samir's plan? *300 minutes*
2. How many minutes did Samir use this month? _____
3. How much is Samir's basic plan? _____
4. How much did Samir pay for additional minutes? _____

C Answer the questions. Use your own information.

1. When do you usually talk on the phone? _____
2. How long do you usually talk on the phone? _____

Name: _____

Lesson F Another view

A Look at the cell phone calling plans. Answer the questions.

Phone Calling Plans			
Name	*Cost*	*Monthly minutes*	*Additional minutes*
Plan A	$24 a month	100	$0.10
Plan B	$58 a month	300	$0.25
Plan C	$69 a month	600	$0.32

1. How much is Plan A every month? ____*$24*____

2. How much is Plan C every month? _____

3. How many monthly minutes does Plan B have? _____

4. How many monthly minutes does Plan C have? _____

5. How much is one additional minute with Plan A? _____

B Look at the phone bill. Read the answers. Write questions.

TALK TIME Phone Bill

Samir Patel
4555 Washington St.
Los Angeles, CA 90040

Phone number: (323) 555-0989
Account number: 8099-0989
Billing date: January 15, 2008

	Monthly minutes	Calling charges
Monthly plan – Plan B	300	$58
Additional minutes	20	$5
Total	320	$63

1. How many *minutes come with Samir's plan?* _____ 300 minutes

2. How many _____ 320 minutes

3. How much _____ $58

4. How much _____ $5

C Answer the questions. Use your own information.

1. When do you usually talk on the phone? _____

2. How long do you usually talk on the phone? _____

3. Who do you usually talk to? _____

Unit 4 Health

Name: _____

Lesson A *Get ready*

A Match the pictures with the words.

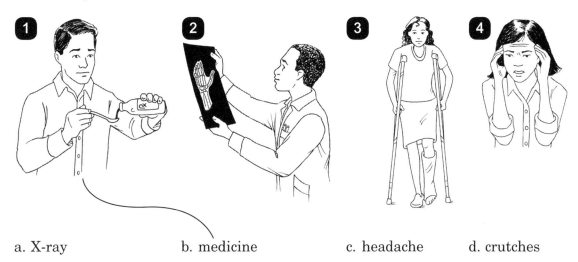

a. X-ray   b. medicine   c. headache   d. crutches

B Read the note. Circle the correct sentences.

> Hi Osman,
>   I had an accident at work, and I hurt my leg. The doctor took an X-ray. My leg is not broken, but I have to stay at the hospital this afternoon. I need you to pick up my son, Rashid, from school when you pick up your son. My wife, Noor, will pick me up from the hospital later. Thank you so much for your help!
>   Ali

1. (Ali hurt his leg.)   Osman hurt his leg.

2. Rashid needed an X-ray.   Ali needed an X-ray.

3. Osman's son is Rashid.   Ali's son is Rashid.

4. Ali has to stay at the hospital.   Ali has to stay at home.

5. Osman will pick up Ali from the hospital.   Noor will pick up Ali from the hospital.

C Write places where accidents happen.

1. *in the kitchen* _____   3. _____

2. _____   4. _____

Lesson A *Get ready*

A Look at the pictures. Complete the sentences.

| crutches | headache | medicine | X-ray |

1. He is taking   2. He is holding an   3. She is on   4. She has a

medicine .   _____ .   _____ .   _____ .

B Read the note. Complete the sentences.

> Hi Osman,
>
> I had an accident at work, and I hurt my leg. The doctor took an X-ray. My leg is not broken, but I have to stay at the hospital this afternoon. I need you to pick up my son, Rashid, from school when you pick up your son. My wife, Noor, will pick me up from the hospital later. Thank you so much for your help!
>
> Ali

1. Ali _____ hurt _____ his leg.

2. _____ needed an X-ray.

3. Ali's son is _____ .

4. Ali has to stay at the _____ .

5. _____ will pick up Ali from the hospital.

C Write three places where accidents happen and three dangerous jobs.

Accidents happen	Dangerous jobs
1. *in the kitchen*	1.
2.	2.
3.	3.

56   Add Ventures 2

Lesson A *Get ready*

Name: _____

A Look at the pictures. Complete the sentences.

1. He is *taking* _____
   medicine _____ .

2. He is _____
   _____ .

3. She is _____
   _____ .

4. She has _____
   _____ .

B Read the note. Answer the questions. Write complete sentences.

Hi Osman,
   I had an accident at work, and I hurt my leg. The doctor took an X-ray. My leg is not broken, but I have to stay at the hospital this afternoon. I need you to pick up my son, Rashid, from school when you pick up your son. My wife, Noor, will pick me up from the hospital later. Thank you so much for your help!
                                                                                 Ali

1. What happened to Ali? *Ali hurt his leg.* _____

2. Who needed an X-ray? _____

3. What is Ali's son's name? _____

4. Where does Ali have to stay? _____

5. Who will pick up Ali from the hospital? _____

C Write four places where accidents happen and four dangerous jobs.

Accidents happen	Dangerous jobs
1. *in the kitchen*	1.
2.	2.
3.	3.
4.	4.

Unit 4 Health

Lesson B *What do I have to do?*

Name: _____

A Match the pictures with the warnings.

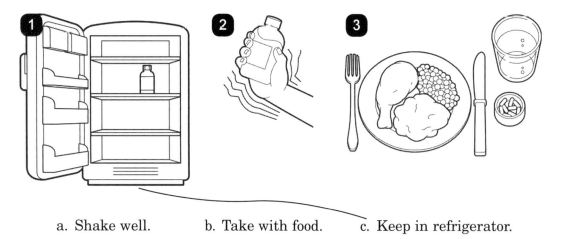

    a. Shake well.   b. Take with food.   c. Keep in refrigerator.

B Circle the correct verb.

1. What **do** / **does** she have to do?   She **has to** / **have to** get an X-ray.
2. What **do** / **does** he have to do?   He **has to** / **have to** go to the hospital.
3. What **do** / **does** I have to do?   You **has to** / **have to** use crutches.
4. What **do** / **does** they have to do?   They **has to** / **have to** take their medicine.
5. What **do** / **does** we have to do?   We **has to** / **have to** see a doctor.

C Complete the conversation.

| Here's your prescription.   I understand.   You have to stay in bed |

Doctor You have the flu.

You What do I have to do?

Doctor *You have to stay in bed* _____ for three days.

You Oh, OK.

Doctor _____ You have

to take it in the morning.

You Do I have to keep this medicine in the refrigerator?

Doctor No, you don't. But keep it out of reach of children.

You _____

© Cambridge University Press 2008 **Photocopiable**

Lesson B *What do I have to do?*

Name: _____

A Complete the warning labels.

Take	Keep	Shake

___*Keep*___ in refrigerator.   _____ well.   _____ with food.

B Complete the sentences. Use *do* or *does*, and *have to* or *has to*.

1. What ___*does*___ she have to do?   She ___*has to*___ get an X-ray.
2. What _____ he have to do?   He _____ go to hospital.
3. What _____ I have to do?   You _____ use crutches.
4. What _____ they have to do?   They _____ take their medicine.
5. What _____ we have to do?   We _____ see a doctor.

C Complete the conversation.

Here's your prescription.	I understand.	You have to stay in bed
in the morning	of children	

Doctor You have the flu.

You What do I have to do?

Doctor ___*You have to stay in bed*_____ for three days.

You Oh, OK.

Doctor _____ You have to take it

_____ .

You Do I have to keep this medicine in the refrigerator?

Doctor No, you don't. But keep it out of reach _____ .

You _____

Add Ventures 2   **59**

Name: _____

Lesson B *What do I have to do?*

A Look at the pictures. Complete the warning labels.

_____Keep_____ in refrigerator.   _____ well.   _____ with food.

B Complete the sentences. Use *do* or *does*, and *have to* or *has to*.

1. What _does she have to do_____ ? She _____has to_____ get an X-ray.
2. What _____ ? He _____ go to the hospital.
3. What _____ ? You _____ use crutches.
4. What _____ ? They _____ take their medicine.
5. What _____ ? We _____ see a doctor.

C Complete the conversation.

Call me	Here's your prescription.	I understand.	You have to stay in bed
flu	in the morning	of children	

Doctor You have the _flu_____ .

You What do I have to do?

Doctor _____ for three days.

You Oh, OK.

Doctor _____ You have to take it

_____ .

You Do I have to keep this medicine in the refrigerator?

Doctor No, you don't. But keep it out of reach _____ .

You _____

Doctor _____ if you have any questions.

Lesson C *You should go to the hospital.*

A Match the questions with the answers.

1. My stomach hurts. ⎯⎯⎯⎯   a. What should she do?

2. His leg hurts.   b. What should I do?

3. She has a sprained ankle.   c. What should they do?

4. Their eyes hurt.   d. What should he do?

B Circle the correct advice.

1. Your tooth hurts. You should ___ .   (a. see a dentist)   b. drink some water

2. Your eyes hurt. You should ___ .   a. stay in the sun   b. rest

3. You have a headache. You should ___ .   a. take some aspirin   b. see a dentist

4. You hurt your leg. You should ___ .   a. stay in the shade   b. get an X-ray

5. You are very hot. You should ___ .   a. see a doctor   b. stay in the shade

C Unscramble the words. Complete the conversations.

1.   **You** (leg / hurts / My / .) _My leg hurts._ _____

          (I / What should / do / ?) _____

    Friend (rest / You / should / .) _____

          (walk / shouldn't / You / .) _____

2.   **You** (My mother / feel well / doesn't / .) _____

          (What / she / do / should / ?) _____

    Friend (a break / take / She should / .) _____

          (shouldn't stay / in the sun / She / .) _____

    You (I'll / her / tell / OK, / .) _____

Name: _____

Lesson C *You should go to the hospital.*

A Complete the questions.

1. My stomach hurts.   What _____*should I*_____ do?

2. His leg hurts.   What _____ do?

3. She has a sprained ankle. What _____ do?

4. Their eyes hurt.   What _____ do?

B Complete the chart with the best advice.

get an X-ray   rest   see a dentist   stay in the shade   take some aspirin

Problem	Advice
1. Your tooth hurts.	*You should see a dentist.*
2. Your eyes hurt.	
3. You have a headache.	
4. You hurt your leg.	
5. You are very hot.	

C Unscramble the words. Complete the conversations.

1. **You** (leg / hurts / My / .) _*My leg hurts.*_____

   (should / I / What / do / ?) _____

   Friend (You / should / rest / .) _____

   (walk / shouldn't / You / .) _____

2. **You** (mother / My / feel / doesn't / well / .) _____

   (What / she / do / should / ?) _____

   Friend (break / take / a / should / She / .) _____

   (shouldn't / sun / stay / the / She / in / .) _____

   You (I'll / her / tell / OK, / .) _____

Name: _____

Lesson C *You should go to the hospital.*

A Write questions. Use *What*.

1. My stomach hurts. *What should I do?*

2. His leg hurts. _____

3. She has a sprained ankle. _____

4. Their eyes hurt. _____

B Complete the chart. Use some advice more than once.

drink some water	go to the hospital	see a dentist	take a break
get an X-ray	rest	stay in the shade	take some aspirin

Problem	Advice (1)	Advice (2)
1. Your tooth hurts.	*You should see a dentist.*	*You should take some aspirin.*
2. Your eyes hurt.		
3. You have a headache.		
4. You hurt your leg.		
5. You are very hot.		

C Unscramble the words. Complete the conversations.

1. **You** (leg / hurts / My / .) *My leg hurts.* _____

   (should / I / What / do / ?) _____

   Friend (You / should / rest / .) _____

   (walk / shouldn't / You / .) _____

   (You / get / X-ray / should / an / .) _____

2. **You** (mother / My / feel / doesn't / well / .) _____

   (What / she / do / should / ?) _____

   Friend (break / take / a / should / She / .) _____

   (shouldn't / sun / stay / the / She / in / .) _____

   (should / drink / of / lots / She / water / .) _____

   You (I'll / her / tell / OK, / .) _____

Unit 4 Health

Lesson D *Reading*

Name: _____

A Complete the conversations.

allergies	cut	pains	pressure	rash	sprained

1. **A** Do you have any _a_ _l_ _l_ _e_ _r_ _g_ _i_ _e_ _s_ ?

   B Yes, milk.

2. **A** I think I have a ___ ___ ___ ___ ___ ___ ___ ___ ankle.

   B You should get an X-ray.

3. **A** My dad had chest ___ ___ ___ ___ ___ last night.

   B How is he feeling today?

4. **A** Your hand is red!

   B Yes, I have a ___ ___ ___ ___ .

5. **A** How's my blood ___ ___ ___ ___ ___ ___ ___ ___ today?

   B It's high.

6. **A** I have a bad ___ ___ ___ on my finger.

   B I'll get a bandage for you.

B Which sentences are about using a ladder? Write *A*. Which sentences are about taking medicine? Write *B*.

1. _A_ Never stand on the top step.
2. ___ Take with food.
3. ___ Shake well.
4. ___ Don't carry a lot of equipment while climbing.
5. ___ Keep in the refrigerator.
6. ___ Take in the morning.

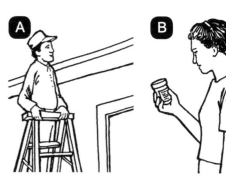

C Circle *should* or *shouldn't*.

1. Never stand on the top step of a ladder. You **should** / (**shouldn't**) stand on the top step.

2. Always take this with food. You **should** / **shouldn't** take this with food.

3. When you climb a ladder, wear a tool belt. You **should** / **shouldn't** wear a tool belt.

4. Keep out of reach of children. You **should** / **shouldn't** keep this away from children.

Name: _____

Lesson **D** *Reading*

A Complete the conversations.

allergies	cut	pains	pressure	rash	sprained

1. **A** Do you have any _____*allergies*_____ ?

   B Yes, milk.

2. **A** I think I have a _____ ankle.

   B You should get an X-ray.

3. **A** My dad had chest _____ last night.

   B How is he feeling today?

4. **A** Your hand is red!

   B Yes, I have a _____ .

5. **A** How's my blood _____ today?

   B It's high.

6. **A** I have a bad _____ on my finger.

   B I'll get a bandage for you.

B Which sentences are about using a ladder? Write *A*. Which sentences are about taking medicine? Write *B*.

1. _*A*_ Never stand on the top step.

2. ____ Take with food.

3. ____ Shake well.

4. ____ Don't carry a lot of equipment while climbing.

5. ____ Keep in the refrigerator.

6. ____ Take in the morning.

7. ____ Do not freeze.

8. ____ Wear a tool belt while climbing up or down.

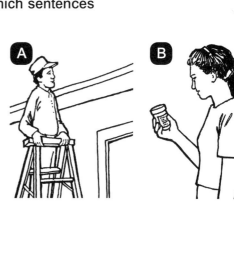

C Complete the sentences. Use *should* or *shouldn't*.

1. Never stand on the top step of a ladder. You _____*shouldn't*_____ stand on the top step.

2. Always take this with food. You _____ take this with food.

3. When you climb a ladder, wear a tool belt. You _____ wear a tool belt.

4. Keep out of reach of children. You _____ keep this away from children.

Lesson D *Reading*

Name: _____

A Complete the conversations.

1. **A** Do you have any a _llergies_____ ?

   B Yes, milk.

2. **A** I think I have a s_____ ankle.

   B You should get an X-ray.

3. **A** My dad had chest p_____ last night.

   B How is he feeling today?

4. **A** Your hand is red!

   B Yes, I have a r_____ .

5. **A** How's my blood p_____ today?

   B It's high.

6. **A** I have a bad c_____ on my finger.

   B I'll get a bandage for you.

B Which sentences are about using a ladder? Write *A*. Which sentences are about taking medicine? Write *B*.

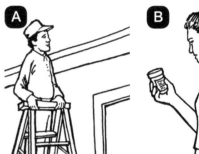

1. _A_ Never stand on the top step.

2. ____ Take with food.

3. ____ Shake well.

4. ____ Don't carry a lot of equipment while climbing.

5. ____ Keep in the refrigerator.

6. ____ Take in the morning.

7. ____ Do not freeze.

8. ____ Wear a tool belt while climbing up or down.

9. ____ Never stand on the shelf.

10. ____ Drink lots of water.

C Write sentences. Use *should* and *shouldn't*.

1. Never stand on the top step of a ladder.

   _You shouldn't stand on the top step._____

2. Always take this with food.

   _____

3. When you climb a ladder, wear a tool belt.

   _____

4. Keep out of reach of children.

   _____

Name: _____

Lesson E *Writing*

A Look at the pictures. Number the sentences in the correct order.

1

_3_ I hurt my back.

_2_ I picked up a heavy box.

_1_ I was at work.

2

____ I fell off a ladder.

____ I was in my house.

____ I have a headache.

3

____ I was in the kitchen.

____ I burned my hand.

____ I picked up a hot pan.

B Read about an accident. Circle the answers.

> Today's date is January 25, 2008. Eduardo Perez was at work yesterday at 8:00 p.m. There was water on the floor. He slipped and hurt his foot. First, he had to go to the hospital. Then, at 11:00 p.m., he completed an accident report form.

1. What day did the accident happen? (a. January 24, 2008) b. January 25, 2008

2. What time did the accident happen? a. 8:00 p.m. b. 11:00 p.m.

3. What happened? a. Eduardo slipped. b. Eduardo hurt his foot.

4. How did the injury happen? a. He slipped. b. He was at work.

C Complete the accident report form. Use the information from Exercise B.

Speedy **D**elivery **C**ompany   **980 South Peach Street**   **Marietta, GA 30060**

ACCIDENT REPORT FORM

Employee name: _Eduardo Perez_ _____

Date of accident: _____   Time: _____

How did the accident happen? _I was_ _____ . _There was water on the floor_ .

I slipped and _____ . _I had to go to the_ _____ .

A Look at the pictures. Complete the sentences and number them in the correct order.

| at work | back | hand | headache | kitchen | ladder |

1 **2** **3**

___ I hurt my _____ .   ___ I fell off a _____ .   ___ I was in the _____ .

___ I picked up a heavy box.   ___ I was in my house.   ___ I burned my _____ .

1 I was *at work* _____ . ___ I have a _____ .   ___ I picked up a hot pan.

B Read about an accident. Answer the questions.

> Today's date is January 25, 2008. Eduardo Perez was at work yesterday at 8:00 p.m. There was water on the floor. He slipped and hurt his foot. First, he had to go to the hospital. Then, at 11:00 p.m., he completed an accident report form.

1. What day did the accident happen? *January 24, 2008*

2. What time did the accident happen? _____

3. What happened? _____

4. How did the injury happen? _____

C Complete the accident report form. Use the information from Exercise B.

Speedy **D**elivery **C**ompany   **980 South Peach Street**   **Marietta, GA 30060**

ACCIDENT REPORT FORM

Employee name: *Eduardo Perez* _____

Date of accident: _____   Time: _____

How did the accident happen? *I was at work. . . .* _____

_____

A Look at the pictures. Complete the sentences and number them in the correct order.

1

___ I hurt my _____ .
___ I picked up a heavy box.
_1_ I was *at work* .

2

___ I fell off a _____ .
___ I was in my house.
___ I have a _____ .

3

___ I was in the _____ .
___ I burned my _____ .
___ I picked up a hot pan.

B Read about an accident. Read the answers. Complete the questions.

> Today's date is January 25, 2008. Eduardo Perez was at work yesterday at 8:00 p.m. There was water on the floor. He slipped and hurt his foot. First, he had to go to the hospital. Then, at 11:00 p.m., he completed an accident report form.

1. What *day did the accident happen* ? January 24, 2008
2. What _____ ? 8:00 p.m.
3. What _____ ? Eduardo hurt his foot.
4. How _____ ? He slipped.

C Complete the accident report form. Use the information from Exercise B.

Speedy **D**elivery **C**ompany   **980 South Peach Street   Marietta, GA 30060**
ACCIDENT REPORT FORM

Employee name: *Eduardo Perez* _____

Date of accident: _____   Time: _____

How did the accident happen? _____

_____

Name: _____

Lesson F · Another view

A Look at the medicine label. Circle the answers.

Drug facts
Active ingredient (in each tablet)   **Purpose**
Ibuprofen 200 mg . . . . Pain reliever
Uses Temporary relief of headaches, toothaches, colds, and backaches
Warning
Do not use if you have allergies to pain relievers.
Directions
Adults and children 12 years and over: Take 1 tablet every 4 to 6 hours. Do not take more than 6 tablets in 24 hours. Do not give to children under 12. Do not take more than directed.

1. Why should you take this medicine?

   a. for high blood pressure

   b. for allergies

   (c. for headaches)

2. How many tablets should children under 12 take?

   a. no tablets

   b. one tablet

   c. four tablets

3. How many tablets should an adult take at one time?

   a. no tablets

   b. one tablet

   c. four tablets

4. How many tablets can an adult take in one day?

   a. six tablets

   b. seven tablets

   c. eight tablets

B Read the clues. Complete the puzzle.

blood	cut	hospital	label	report

Down

1. She has high _____ pressure.
2. He has to fill out an accident _____ .
3. The knife slipped, and she has a bad _____ .
5. Always read the warning _____ .

Across

4. I went to the _____ for an X-ray.

© Cambridge University Press 2008 **Photocopiable**

Name: _____

Lesson F *Another view*

A Look at the medicine label. Circle the answers.

Drug facts
Active ingredient (in each tablet)   **Purpose**
Ibuprofen 200 mg . . . . Pain reliever
Uses Temporary relief of headaches, toothaches, colds, and backaches
Warning
Do not use if you have allergies to pain relievers.
Directions
Adults and children 12 years and over: Take 1 tablet every 4 to 6 hours. Do not take more than 6 tablets in 24 hours. Do not give to children under 12. Do not take more than directed.

1. Why should you take this medicine?

   a. for high blood pressure

   b. for allergies

   (c. for headaches)

   d. for chest pains

2. How many tablets should children under 12 take?

   a. no tablets

   b. one tablet

   c. four tablets

   d. six tablets

3. How many tablets should an adult take at one time?

   a. no tablets

   b. one tablet

   c. four tablets

   d. six tablets

4. How many tablets can an adult take in one day?

   a. six tablets

   b. seven tablets

   c. eight tablets

   d. twelve tablets

B Read the clues. Complete the puzzle.

Down

1. She has high _____ pressure.
2. He has to fill out an accident _____ .
3. The knife slipped, and she has a bad _____ .
5. Always read the warning _____ .

Across

4. I went to the _____ for an X-ray.

(Crossword grid: 1 down "b l o o d", 2 down "r", 3 down "c", 4 across "h o ...", 5 down "l")

A Look at the medicine label. Answer the questions.

Drug facts	
Active ingredient (in each tablet)	**Purpose**
Ibuprofen 200 mg . . . . Pain reliever	
Uses Temporary relief of headaches, toothaches, colds, and backaches	
Warning	
Do not use if you have allergies to pain relievers.	
Directions	
Adults and children 12 years and over: Take 1 tablet every 4 to 6 hours. Do not take more than 6 tablets in 24 hours. Do not give to children under 12. Do not take more than directed.	

1. Why should you take this medicine?

   You should take this medicine for headaches, toothaches, colds, and backaches.

2. How many tablets should children under 12 take?

   _____

3. How many tablets should an adult take at one time?

   _____

4. How many tablets can an adult take in one day?

   _____

B Read the clues. Complete the puzzle.

Down

1. She has high _____ pressure.
2. He has to fill out an accident _____ .
3. The knife slipped, and she has a bad _____ .
5. Always read the warning _____ .

Across

3. If you have _____ , you should stay in bed and rest.
4. I went to the _____ for an X-ray.
6. Take 1 _____ every 12 hours.

Lesson A *Get ready*

A Look at the picture. Write the words.

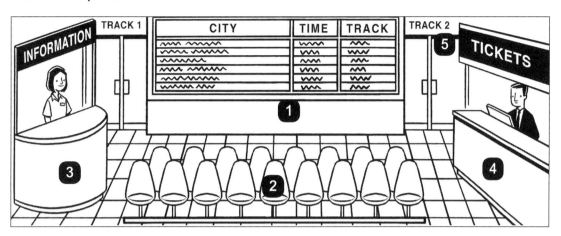

| departure board | information desk | ticket booth | track number | waiting area |

1.   d _e_ _p_ _a_ _r_ |_t_| _u_ _r_ _e_   b _o_ _a_ _r_ _d_

2. w __ __ __ __ __ __   a |__| __ __

3.   i __ __ __ __ __ |__| __ __ __ __   d __ __ __

4.   t |__| __ __ __ __   b __ __ __ __ __

5.   t __ __ __ __ |__| __ __ __ __ __ __

What word do the boxes spell? _____

B Read the train information. Match the questions with the answers.

Departures		
City	**Time**	**Track**
Washington, D.C.	9:00	1
New York City	10:00	3
Boston	11:00	2

1. What time does the train to Washington, D.C., leave?   a. Track 1

2. What time does the train to Boston leave?   b. Track 2

3. What time does the train to New York City leave?   c. 10:00

4. What track does the train to Washington, D.C., leave from?   d. 9:00

5. What track does the train to Boston leave from?   e. 11:00

Name: _____

Lesson A *Get ready*

A Look at the picture. Write the words.

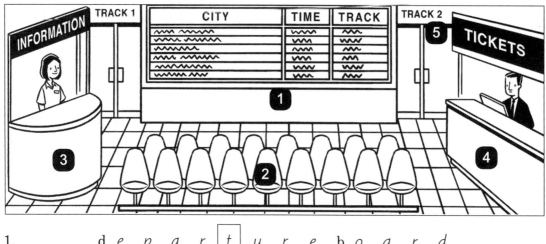

1. d_e_ _p_ _a_ _r_ |t| _u_ _r_ _e_ b_o_ _a_ _r_ _d_

2. w___ ___ ___ ___ ___ ___   a| |___ ___

3.   i___ ___ ___ ___ ___ | |___ ___ ___ ___   d___ ___ ___

4.   t| |___ ___ ___ ___   b___ ___ ___ ___

5.   t___ ___ ___ ___ | |___ ___ ___

What word do the boxes spell? _____

B Read the train information. Answer the questions.

Departures		
City	Time	Track
Washington, D.C.	9:00	1
New York City	10:00	3
Boston	11:00	2

1. What time does the train to Washington, D.C., leave? _9:00_ _____

2. What time does the train to Boston leave? _____

3. What time does the train to New York City leave?_____

4. What track does the train to Washington, D.C., leave from? _____

5. What track does the train to Boston leave from? _____

Lesson A *Get ready*

A Look at the picture. Write the words.

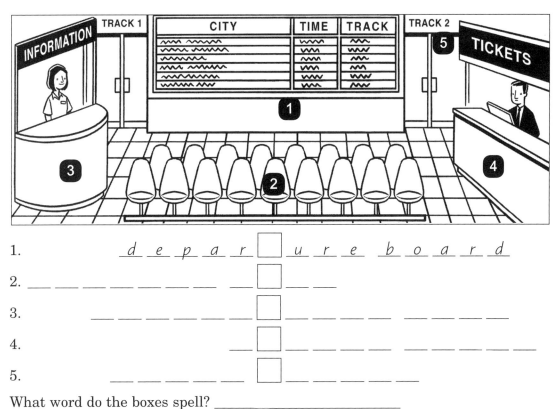

1. _d_ _e_ _p_ _a_ _r_ ☐ _u_ _r_ _e_   _b_ _o_ _a_ _r_ _d_
2. __ __ __ __ __ __ __ ☐ __
3.   __ __ __ __ __ __ __ ☐ __ __ __ __ __ __ __ __
4.   __ __ __ ☐ __ __ __ __ __ __ __
5.   __ __ __ __ __ ☐ __ __ __ __

What word do the boxes spell? _____

B Read the train information. Read the answers. Complete the questions.

Departures		
City	Time	Track
Washington, D.C.	9:00	1
New York City	10:00	3
Boston	11:00	2

1. What time *does the train to Washington, D.C., leave* ? 9:00
2. What time _____ ? 11:00
3. What time _____ ? 10:00
4. What track _____ ? Track 1
5. What track _____ ? Track 2

Add Ventures 2   **75**

Lesson B How often? How long?

A Look at the bus schedule. Circle the answers.

York to City Airport		
Departs	Arrives	Duration
6:00 a.m.	7:40 a.m.	1h 40m
11:00 a.m.	12:40 p.m.	1h 40m
4:00 p.m.	5:40 p.m.	1h 40m

City Airport to York via River Junction		
Departs	Arrives	Duration
8:00 a.m.	10:10 a.m.	2h 10m
1:00 p.m.	3:10 p.m.	2h 10m
6:00 p.m.	8:10 p.m.	2h 10m
7:30 p.m.	9:40 p.m.	2h 10m

1. How often does the bus go from York to City Airport?

   a. three times a day   b. four times a day

2. How long does it take to get from York to City Airport?

   a. one hour and 40 minutes   b. two hours and 10 minutes

3. How often does the bus go from City Airport to York?

   a. three times a day   b. four times a day

4. How long does it take to get from City Airport to York?

   a. one hour and 40 minutes   b. two hours and 10 minutes

5. What time does the 4:00 p.m. bus arrive at City Airport?

   a. 5:40 p.m.   b. 8:10 p.m.

6. What time does the 6:00 p.m. bus arrive in York?

   a. 7:40 p.m.   b. 8:10 p.m.

B Answer the questions. Use your own information.

1. How often do you take the bus to school?

   _____

2. How often do you drive to school?

   _____

Name: _____

Lesson **B** *How often? How long?*

A Look at the bus schedule. Answer the questions.

York to City Airport		
Departs	Arrives	Duration
6:00 a.m.	7:40 a.m.	1h 40m
11:00 a.m.	12:40 p.m.	1h 40m
4:00 p.m.	5:40 p.m.	1h 40m

City Airport to York via River Junction		
Departs	Arrives	Duration
8:00 a.m.	10:10 a.m.	2h 10m
1:00 p.m.	3:10 p.m.	2h 10m
6:00 p.m.	8:10 p.m.	2h 10m
7:30 p.m.	9:40 p.m.	2h 10m

1. How often does the bus go from York to City Airport? *three times a day* _____

2. How long does it take to get from York to City Airport? _____

3. How often does the bus go from City Airport to York? _____

4. How long does it take to get from City Airport to York? _____

5. What time does the 4:00 p.m. bus arrive at City Airport? _____

6. What time does the 6:00 p.m. bus arrive in York? _____

B Answer the questions. Use your own information.

1. How often do you take the bus to school?

_____

2. How often do you drive to school?

_____

3. How often do you cook dinner?

_____

Lesson B *How often? How long?*

A Look at the bus schedule. Read the answers. Complete the questions.

York to City Airport		
Departs	**Arrives**	**Duration**
6:00 a.m.	7:40 a.m.	1h 40m
11:00 a.m.	12:40 p.m.	1h 40m
4:00 p.m.	5:40 p.m.	1h 40m

City Airport to York via River Junction		
Departs	**Arrives**	**Duration**
8:00 a.m.	10:10 a.m.	2h 10m
1:00 p.m.	3:10 p.m.	2h 10m
6:00 p.m.	8:10 p.m.	2h 10m
7:30 p.m.	9:40 p.m.	2h 10m

1. How often does the bus go from _____*York*_____ to City Airport? three times a day

2. How long does it take to get from _____ to City Airport? one hour and 40 minutes

3. How often does the bus go from _____ to York? four times a day

4. How long does it take to get from City Airport to _____ ? two hours and ten minutes

5. What time does the _____ bus arrive at City Airport? 5:40 p.m.

6. What time does the _____ bus arrive in York? 8:10 p.m.

B Answer the questions. Use your own information.

1. How often do you take the bus to school?

_____

2. How often do you drive to school?

_____

3. How often do you cook dinner?

_____

4. How often do you go on vacation?

_____

Name: _____

Lesson C *She often walks to school.*

A Look at the chart. Ben, Lenka, and Sushila go to school five days a week.
Circle the best answers.

	Ben	Lenka	Sushila
	2 times a week	1 time a week	5 times a week
	3 times a week	0 times a week	0 times a week
	0 times a week	4 times a week	0 times a week

1. How often does Ben take the bus to school?   usually / (never)
2. How often does Ben drive to school?   often / rarely
3. How often does Lenka ride her bike to school?   often / rarely
4. How often does Lenka take the bus to school?   usually / rarely
5. How often does Sushila ride her bike to school? always / sometimes
6. How often does Sushila drive to school?   often / never

B Rewrite the sentences. Use adverbs of frequency.

1. Omar comes to class. (always) *Omar always comes to class.* _____

2. He is late. (rarely) _____

3. He comes with his friend Paolo. (sometimes) _____

4. They take the bus. (usually) _____

C Answer the questions. Use adverbs of frequency and your own information.

1. How often do you come to class? _____

2. How often are you late for class? _____

3. How often do you drive a car? _____

Add Ventures 2

Name: _____

Lesson C *She often walks to school.*

A Look at the chart. Ben, Lenka, and Sushila go to school five days a week.
Circle the best answers.

	Ben	Lenka	Sushila
🚲	2 times a week	1 time a week	5 times a week
🚗	3 times a week	0 times a week	0 times a week
🚌	0 times a week	4 times a week	0 times a week

1. How often does Ben take the bus to school?   usually / sometimes / (never)

2. How often does Ben drive to school?   often / rarely / never

3. How often does Lenka ride her bike to school?   often / rarely / never

4. How often does Lenka take the bus to school?   always / usually / rarely

5. How often does Sushila ride her bike to school?   always / sometimes / rarely

6. How often does Sushila drive to school?   always / often / never

B Unscramble the words. Write the sentences.

1. Omar / comes / to class / always *Omar always comes to class.* _____

2. He / late / rarely / is _____

3. He / comes / with / sometimes / his friend Paolo _____

4. They / take the bus / usually _____

C Write sentences. Use adverbs of frequency and your own information.

1. How often do you come to class? _____

2. How often are you late for class? _____

3. How often do you drive a car? _____

4. How often do you ride a bike? _____

© Cambridge University Press 2008 **Photocopiable**

Name: _____

Lesson C *She often walks to school.*

A Look at the chart. Ben, Lenka, and Sushila go to school five days a week.
Answer the questions. Use adverbs of frequency.

	Ben	**Lenka**	**Sushila**
🚲	2 times a week	1 time a week	5 times a week
🚗	3 times a week	0 times a week	0 times a week
🚌	0 times a week	4 times a week	0 times a week

1. How often does Ben take the bus to school? *Ben never takes the bus to school.*

2. How often does Ben drive to school? _____

3. How often does Lenka ride her bike to school? _____

4. How often does Lenka take the bus to school? _____

5. How often does Sushila ride her bike to school? _____

6. How often does Sushila drive to school? _____

B Answer the questions about Omar. Use the words in parentheses.

1. How often does Omar come to class? (always) *Omar always comes to class.*

2. How often is he late? (rarely) _____

3. How often does Omar come with his friend Paolo? (sometimes) _____

4. How often do they take the bus? (usually) _____

C Write sentences. Use adverbs of frequency and your own information.

1. (come to class) _____

2. (late for class) _____

3. (drive a car) _____

4. (ride a bike) _____

Lesson D *Reading*

Name: _____

A Match the pictures with the words.

a. stay at a hotel   b. go sightseeing   c. write postcards   d. buy souvenirs

B Read the note. Circle the answers.

> *Dear Lela,*
> *My mother and I usually take a trip together once a year. This year, we are visiting Boston. Yesterday, we went to Boston Common (a park), and we went shopping. We took a lot of pictures. Tomorrow, we want to go on a sightseeing bus trip around Boston. It takes about three hours.*
>
> *Your friend,*
> *Miriam*

1. How often do Miriam and her mother go on trips?   often / (rarely)

2. When did they go shopping?   yesterday / today

3. When do they want to go sightseeing?   today / tomorrow

4. How long does the sightseeing bus trip take?   three hours / four hours

C Write three things you usually do on a trip.

1. _____

2. _____

3. _____

Name: _____

Lesson D *Reading*

A Look at the pictures. Write the words.

| buy souvenirs | go sightseeing | stay at a hotel | write postcards |

__*write postcards*__   _____   _____   _____

B Read the note. Answer the questions.

> Dear Lela,
>
>   My mother and I usually take a trip together once a year. This year, we are visiting Boston. Yesterday, we went to Boston Common (a park), and we went shopping. We took a lot of pictures. Tomorrow, we want to go on a sightseeing bus trip around Boston. It takes about three hours.
>
> Your friend,
> Miriam

1. How often do Miriam and her mother go on trips? __*They rarely go on trips.*__

2. When did they go shopping? _____

3. When do they want to go sightseeing? _____

4. How long does the sightseeing bus trip take? _____

C Write four things you usually do on a trip.

1. _____

2. _____

3. _____

4. _____

Lesson D *Reading*

Name: _____

A Look at the pictures. Write the words.

write *postcards*   buy _____   go _____   stay at a _____

B Read the postcard. Read the answers. Complete the questions.

> Dear Lela,
>   My mother and I usually take a trip together once a year. This year, we are visiting Boston. Yesterday, we went to Boston Common (a park), and we went shopping. We took a lot of pictures. Tomorrow, we want to go on a sightseeing bus trip around Boston. It takes about three hours.
>
> Your friend,
> Miriam

1. How often *do Miriam and her mother go on trips* ?   They rarely go on trips.

2. When _____ ?   They went shopping yesterday.

3. When _____ ?   They want to go sightseeing tomorrow.

4. How long _____ ?   It takes about three hours.

C Write three sentences about things you usually do on a trip.

1. _____

2. _____

3. _____

Lesson **E** *Writing*

A Read about Soledad's trip. Match the questions with the answers.

> Soledad took a trip to Canada. She visited her brother and his wife. They live in Toronto. She usually visits them twice a year. It takes about five hours to drive there from Cleveland. This year, she visited Niagara Falls and went hiking. It was fun.

1. Where did Soledad go?
2. Who did she visit?
3. How often does she go there?
4. How long does it take to get there?
5. What did she do there?

a. She goes there twice a year.
b. It takes five hours.
c. She visited Niagara Falls.
d. She went to Canada.
e. She visited her brother and his wife.

B Complete the letter to a friend. Write about a trip you took to visit your family or a friend.

> Dear _____ ,
>
>   How are you? I'm fine. I just got back from a trip to _____ .
>   (name of place)
> I went to visit _____ . _____ lives / live in
>   (friend or family member)   (He / She / They)
> _____ . I usually visit _____ _____ a year. It
>   (name of place)   (him / her / them) (number of times)
> takes about _____ to get there.
>   (number of hours)
> Your friend,
>
> _____

Lesson **E** *Writing*

A Read about Soledad's trip. Answer the questions.

> Soledad took a trip to Canada. She visited her brother and his wife. They live in Toronto. She usually visits them twice a year. It takes about five hours to drive there from Cleveland. This year, she visited Niagara Falls and went hiking. It was fun.

1. Where did Soledad go? *She went to Canada.* _____

2. Who did she visit? _____

3. How often does she go there? _____

4. How long does it take to get there? _____

5. What did she do there? _____

B Complete the letter to a friend. Write about a trip you took to visit your family or a friend.

> *Dear* _____ ,
>
>   *How are you? I'm fine. I just got back from a trip to* _____ .
>   (name of place)
> *I went to visit* _____ . _____ *lives / live in*
>   (friend or family member)   (He / She / They)
> _____ . *I usually visit* _____ _____ *a year.*
>   (name of place)   (him / her / them) (number of times)
> *It takes about* _____ *to get there by* _____ . *We*
>   (number of hours)   (plane / car / bus / train)
> _____ .
>   (What did you do?)
> *Your friend,*
>
> _____

Lesson E *Writing*

A Read about Soledad's trip. Read the answers. Complete the questions.

> Soledad took a trip to Canada. She visited her brother and his wife. They live in Toronto. She usually visits them twice a year. It takes about five hours to drive there from Cleveland. This year, she visited Niagara Falls and went hiking. It was fun.

1. Where *did Soledad go* _____? She went to Canada.

2. Who _____? She visited her brother and his wife.

3. How often _____? She goes there twice a year.

4. How long _____? It takes five hours.

5. What _____? She visited Niagara Falls.

B Complete the letter to a friend. Write about a trip you took to visit your family or a friend.

> Dear _____ ,
>
> How are you? I'm fine. I just got back from a trip to _____ .
>   (name of place)
> I went to visit _____ . _____ lives / live in
>   (friend or family member) (He / She / They)
> _____ . I usually visit _____ _____ a year.
> (name of place)   (him / her / them) (number of times)
> It takes about _____ to get there by _____ . We
>   (number of hours)   (plane / car / bus / train)
> _____ , and we _____ .
> (What did you do?)   (What else did you do?)
>
> Your friend,
>
> _____

A Look at the bus schedule. Circle the answers.

Bus Schedule (Weekdays)

Main St.	Park Ave.	Pine St.	Maple St.	Walnut St.	Elm St.
6:08 a.m.	6:10 a.m.	6:15 a.m.	6:20 a.m.	6:23 a.m.	6:26 a.m.
6:38 a.m.	6:40 a.m.	6:45 a.m.	6:50 a.m.	6:53 a.m.	6:56 a.m.
7:08 a.m.	7:10 a.m.	7:15 a.m.	7:20 a.m.	7:23 a.m.	7:26 a.m.
7:15 a.m.	7:17 a.m.	7:22 a.m.	7:27 a.m.	does not stop	does not stop
7:20 a.m. express	7:22 a.m.	does not stop	does not stop	does not stop	7:34 a.m.
7:37 a.m. express	does not stop	does not stop	does not stop	does not stop	7:50 a.m.

1. How long does it take the 7:08 a.m. bus to go from Main St. to Elm St.?

   a. 18 minutes   b. 20 minutes   c. 22 minutes

2. How often does the express bus leave from Main St.?

   a. once a day   b. twice a day   c. three times a day

3. How long does it take the 7:37 a.m. bus to go from Main St. to Elm St.?

   a. 13 minutes   b. 15 minutes   c. 18 minutes

4. How often does the bus go from Pine St. to Walnut St. in the morning?

   a. twice   b. three times   c. four times

5. How many buses stop at Maple St. before 7:00 a.m.?

   a. one   b. two   c. three

B Find the words.

hotel	postcard	souvenir	suitcase	swimming	trip

s	u	i	t	c	a	s	e	b	r	d
o	q	w	d	h	m	r	i	f	x	e
u	t	u	g	o	c	h	b	c	d	h
v	r	k	e	q	u	o	a	e	l	j
e	i	r	p	o	s	t	c	a	r	d
n	p	f	h	v	j	e	h	l	a	o
i	e	m	p	n	y	l	o	k	d	n
r	v	s	w	i	m	m	i	n	g	z

Unit 5 Around town

Lesson F *Another view*

Name: _____

A Look at the bus schedule. Circle the answers.

Bus Schedule (Weekdays)						
Main St.	Park Ave.	Pine St.	Warren St.	Maple St.	Walnut St.	Elm St.
6:08 a.m.	6:10 a.m.	6:15 a.m.	6:18 a.m.	6:20 a.m.	6:23 a.m.	6:26 a.m.
6:38 a.m.	6:40 a.m.	6:45 a.m.	6:48 a.m.	6:50 a.m.	6:53 a.m.	6:56 a.m.
7:08 a.m.	7:10 a.m.	7:15 a.m.	7:20 a.m.	7:20 a.m.	7:23 a.m.	7:26 a.m.
7:15 a.m.	7:17 a.m.	7:22 a.m.	7:30 a.m.	7:27 a.m.	does not stop	does not stop
7:20 a.m. express	7:22 a.m.	does not stop	does not stop	does not stop	does not stop	7:34 a.m.
7:37 a.m. express	does not stop	does not stop	does not stop	does not stop	does not stop	7:50 a.m.

1. How long does it take the 7:08 a.m. bus to go from Main St. to Elm St.?

    a. 17 minutes   (b. 18 minutes)   c. 20 minutes   d. 22 minutes

2. How often does the express bus leave from Main St.?

    a. once a day   b. twice a day   c. three times a day   d. four times a day

3. How long does it take the 7:37 a.m. bus to go from Main St. to Elm St.?

    a. 13 minutes   b. 15 minutes   c. 18 minutes   d. 19 minutes

4. How often does the bus go from Pine St. to Walnut St. in the morning?

    a. twice   b. three times   c. four times   d. six times

5. How many buses stop at Maple St. before 7:00 a.m.?

    a. one   b. two   c. three   d. four

B Find the words.

hotel	postcard	sightseeing	suitcase	trip
plane	shopping	souvenir	swimming	vacation

s	u	i	t	c	a	s	e	b	r	d	s	a
o	q	v	a	c	a	t	i	o	n	e	h	b
u	t	u	g	o	c	h	b	c	d	h	o	c
v	r	k	e	q	u	o	a	e	l	j	p	d
e	i	r	p	o	s	t	c	a	r	d	p	r
n	p	l	a	n	e	e	h	l	a	o	i	e
i	e	m	p	n	y	l	o	k	d	n	n	g
r	v	s	w	i	m	m	i	n	g	z	g	p
a	n	b	s	c	o	d	j	e	v	f	r	h
u	m	s	i	g	h	t	s	e	e	i	n	g

Name: _____

Lesson F *Another view*

A Look at the bus schedule. Answer the questions.

Bus Schedule (Weekdays)						
Main St.	Park Ave.	Pine St.	Warren St.	Maple St.	Walnut St.	Elm St.
6:08 a.m.	6:10 a.m.	6:15 a.m.	6:18 a.m.	6:20 a.m.	6:23 a.m.	6:26 a.m.
6:38 a.m.	6:40 a.m.	6:45 a.m.	6:48 a.m.	6:50 a.m.	6:53 a.m.	6:56 a.m.
7:08 a.m.	7:10 a.m.	7:15 a.m.	7:20 a.m.	7:20 a.m.	7:23 a.m.	7:26 a.m.
7:15 a.m.	7:17 a.m.	7:22 a.m.	7:30 a.m.	7:27 a.m.	does not stop	does not stop
7:20 a.m. express	7:22 a.m.	does not stop	does not stop	does not stop	does not stop	7:34 a.m.
7:37 a.m. express	does not stop	does not stop	does not stop	does not stop	does not stop	7:50 a.m.

1. How long does it take the 7:08 a.m. bus to go from Main St. to Elm St.?   *18 minutes*

2. How often does the express bus leave from Main St.? _____

3. How long does it take the 7:37 a.m. bus to go from Main St. to Elm St.? _____

4. How often does the bus go from Pine St. to Walnut St. in the morning? _____

5. How many buses stop at Maple St. before 7:00 a.m.? _____

B Find nine words from the unit.

```
s  u  i  t  c  a  s  e  b  r  d  s  a
o  q  v  a  c  a  t  i  o  n  e  h  b
u  t  u  g  o  c  h  b  c  d  h  o  c
v  r  k  e  q  u  o  a  e  l  j  p  d
e  i  r  p  o  s  t  c  a  r  d  p  r
n  p  l  a  n  e  e  h  l  a  o  i  e
i  e  m  p  n  y  l  o  k  d  n  n  g
r  v  s  w  i  m  m  i  n  g  z  g  p
a  n  b  s  c  o  d  j  e  v  f  r  h
u  m  s  i  g  h  t  s  e  e  i  n  g
```

Lesson A *Get ready*

Name: _____

A Look at the pictures. Write the letter of the picture.

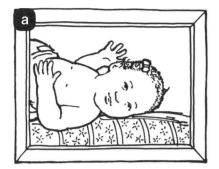

1. Maria was born. _a_

2. Maria started school. _____

3. Maria got her first job. _____

4. Maria graduated from college. _____

5. Maria got married. _____

B Answer the questions. Use your own information.

1. Where were you born?

   I was born in _____ .

2. When did you start school?

   I started school in _____ .

3. When did you move to this country?

   I moved to this country in _____ .

4. When did you start English classes?

   I started English classes in _____ .

5. When did you start your first job?

   I started my first job in _____ .

Name: _____

Lesson A *Get ready*

A Look at the pictures. Write the letter of the picture. Complete the sentences.

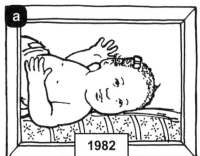

1982

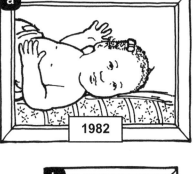

2005

2007

1987

1998

1. _*a*_ Maria was born in ____*1982*____ .

2. ____ Maria started school in _____ .

3. ____ Maria got her first job in _____ .

4. ____ Maria graduated from college in _____ .

5. ____ Maria got married in _____ .

B Answer the questions. Use your own information.

1. Where were you born? _____

2. When did you start school? _____

3. When did you move to this country? _____

4. When did you start English classes? _____

5. When did you start your first job? _____

A Look at the pictures. Write the letter of the picture. Write sentences.

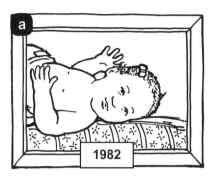

a   1982

b   2005

c   2007

d   1987

e   1998

1. _a_ (born) *Maria was born in 1982.* _____

2. ____ (started school) _____

3. ____ (got first job) _____

4. ____ (graduated from college) _____

5. ____ (got married) _____

B Answer the questions. Use your own information.

1. Where were you born? _____

2. When did you start school? _____

3. When did you move to this country? _____

4. When did you start English classes? _____

5. When did you start your first job? _____

6. When did you start your last job? _____

Name: _____

Lesson B *When did you move here?*

A Write the simple past tense.

1. begin   *b e g a n*
2. finish   __ __ __ __ __ __ __ __
3. have   __ __ __
4. get   __ __ __
5. find   __ __ __ __
6. graduate   __ __ __ __ __ __ __ __ __
7. leave   __ __ __ __
8. study   __ __ __ __ __ __ __
9. meet   __ __ __

B Read about Amir. Match the questions with the answers.

Usha   Amir

Amir's Life

1998: left India
2000: moved to Los Angeles
2003: started college
2005: met Usha
2006: graduated from college
2007: married Usha

1. When did Amir leave India?   a. In 2007.
2. When did Amir move to Los Angeles?   b. In 2006.
3. When did Amir start college?   c. In 1998.
4. When did Amir graduate from college?   d. In 2000.
5. When did Amir meet Usha?   e. In 2003.
6. When did Amir and Usha get married?   f. In 2005.

C Complete the sentences. Use your own information.

1. I left _____ .
2. I moved to _____ .
3. I started _____ .

Unit 6 Time

Name: _____

Lesson B *When did you move here?*

A Write the simple past tense.

1. begin   _____*began*_____
2. finish   _____
3. have   _____
4. get   _____
5. find   _____
6. graduate   _____
7. leave   _____
8. study   _____
9. meet   _____

B Read about Amir. Read the answers. Complete the questions.

Usha   Amir

Amir's Life

1998: left India
2000: moved to Los Angeles
2003: started college
2005: met Usha
2006: graduated from college
2007: married Usha

1. When ___*did*___ Amir _____*leave*_____ India?   In 1998.
2. When _____ Amir _____ to Los Angeles?   In 2000.
3. When _____ Amir _____ college?   In 2003.
4. When _____ Amir _____ from college?   In 2006.
5. When _____ Amir _____ Usha?   In 2005.
6. When _____ Amir and Usha _____ ?   In 2007.

C Complete the sentences. Use your own information.

1. I left _____ .
2. I moved to _____ .
3. I started _____ .
4. I met _____ .

Lesson **B** *When did you move here?*

A Write the simple present tense.

    1. began   _____*begin*_____

    2. finished   _____

    3. had   _____

    4. got   _____

    5. found   _____

    6. graduated _____

    7. left   _____

    8. studied   _____

    9. met   _____

B Read about Amir. Read the answers. Complete the questions.

Usha   Amir

Amir's Life
1998: left India
2000: moved to Los Angeles
2003: started college
2005: met Usha
2006: graduated from college
2007: married Usha

    1. When *did Amir leave India* ? Amir left India in 1998.

    2. When _____ ? Amir moved to Los Angeles in 2000.

    3. When _____ ? Amir started college in 2003.

    4. When _____ ? Amir graduated from college in 2006.

    5. When _____ ? Amir met Usha in 2005.

    6. When _____ ? Amir and Usha got married in 2007.

C Complete the sentences. Use your own information.

    1. I left _____ .

    2. I moved to _____ .

    3. I started _____ .

    4. I met _____ .

Name: _____

Lesson C *He graduated two years ago.*

A Write *in*, *on*, or *at*.

1. ___*in*___ January

2. _____ Tuesday

3. _____ 5:00 p.m.

4. _____ December 3

5. _____ 2007

6. _____ August

7. _____ 2:30 p.m.

8. _____ Friday

9. _____ July 10

B Read about Alicia. Circle the answers.

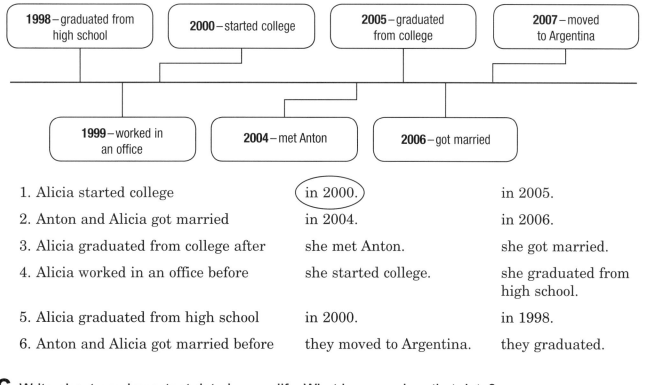

1998 – graduated from high school	**2000** – started college	**2005** – graduated from college	**2007** – moved to Argentina

1999 – worked in an office	**2004** – met Anton	**2006** – got married

1. Alicia started college   (in 2000.)   in 2005.

2. Anton and Alicia got married   in 2004.   in 2006.

3. Alicia graduated from college after   she met Anton.   she got married.

4. Alicia worked in an office before   she started college.   she graduated from high school.

5. Alicia graduated from high school   in 2000.   in 1998.

6. Anton and Alicia got married before   they moved to Argentina.   they graduated.

C Write about one important date in your life. What happened on that date?

On _____ , I _____ .

     Add Ventures 2   **97**

A Write *in*, *on*, or *at*.

1. __*in*__ January
2. _____ Tuesday
3. _____ 5:00 p.m.
4. _____ December 3
5. _____ 2007
6. _____ August

7. _____ 2:30 p.m.
8. _____ Friday
9. _____ July 10
10. _____ 2001
11. _____ September
12. _____ Saturday

B Read about Alicia. Write *T* (true) or *F* (false). Correct the false sentences.

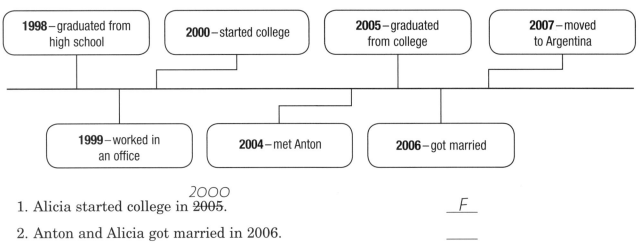

1998 – graduated from high school

2000 – started college

2005 – graduated from college

2007 – moved to Argentina

1999 – worked in an office

2004 – met Anton

2006 – got married

2000
1. Alicia started college in ~~2005~~.   _F_

2. Anton and Alicia got married in 2006.   ____

3. Alicia graduated from college before she met Anton.   ____

4. Alicia worked in an office before she started college.   ____

5. Alicia graduated from high school in 1999.   ____

6. Anton and Alicia got married after they moved to Argentina.   ____

C Write about two important dates in your life. What happened on those dates?

_____

_____

Name: _____

He graduated two years ago.

A Write *in*, *on*, or *at*.

1. __*in*__ January   6. _____ August   11. _____ September

2. _____ Tuesday   7. _____ 2:30 p.m.   12. _____ Saturday

3. _____ 5:00 p.m.   8. _____ Friday   13. _____ Monday

4. _____ December 3   9. _____ July 10   14. _____ 2004

5. _____ 2007   10. _____ 2001   15. _____ 12:30 p.m.

B Read about Alicia. Answer the questions.

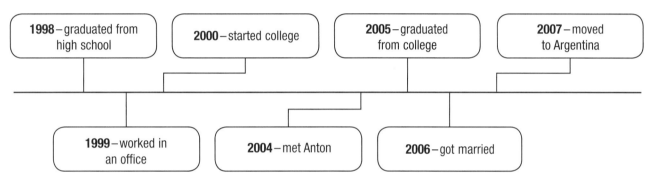

1. When did Alicia start college? *Alicia started college in 2000.* _____

2. When did Anton and Alicia get married? _____

3. What did Alicia do after she met Anton? _____

4. Where did Alicia work before she started college? _____

5. When did Alicia graduate from high school? _____

6. What did Anton and Alicia do before they moved to Argentina? _____

C Write about three important dates in your life. What happened on those dates?

_____

_____

_____

Lesson D *Reading*

Name: _____

A Match the pictures with the words.

a. got married   b. fell in love   c. got a divorce   d. got engaged

B Complete the conversation.

Interviewer: When did you come to the United States?

Keysha: In 1978, I went to college in New York. I _____*studied*_____
                                                          1. (became / studied)
English and accounting. I found a job. I was a waitress in a restaurant. I

_____ my husband there. In 1980, I _____ the
2. (happened / met)   3. (became / took)
restaurant manager.

Interviewer: What _____ after you got married?
                          4. (happened / moved)
Keysha: We _____ the citizenship exam and became U.S.
                    5. (met / took)
citizens. Then we _____ to Chicago. We started our own
                          6. (moved / started)
restaurant.

C Match the questions with the answers. Use the information from Exercise B.

1. When did Keysha move to the United States?

2. When did she become a manager?

3. When did she and her husband become citizens?

4. When did they start a business?

a. They became citizens after they got married.

b. They started a business after they moved to Chicago.

c. She immigrated in 1978.

d. She got promoted in 1980.

Lesson D *Reading*

A Look at the pictures. Complete the sentences. Use the past tense.

| fall in love | get a divorce | get engaged | get married |

 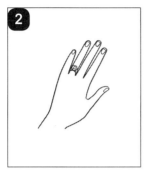  

They ____*fell*____   They _____   They _____   They _____ ____

__*in*____ ____*love*____ .   _____ .   _____ .   _____ .

B Complete the conversation.

| became | happened | met | moved | studied | took |

Interviewer: When did you come to the United States?

Keysha: In 1978, I went to college in New York. I _____*studied*_____
                                                                        1
English and accounting. I found a job. I was a waitress in a restaurant. I

_____ my husband there. In 1980, I _____ the
         2   3
restaurant manager.

Interviewer: What _____ after you got married?
                                      4

Keysha: We _____ the citizenship exam and became U.S.
                         5
citizens. Then we _____ to Chicago. We started our own
                              6
restaurant.

C Write *T* (true) or *F* (false). Correct the false sentences. Use the information
from Exercise B.

          1978

1. Keysha immigrated in ~~1980~~.   ___*F*___

2. She got promoted in 1980.   _____

3. They became citizens before they got married.   _____

4. They started a business before they moved to Chicago. _____

Lesson D *Reading*

A Look at the pictures. Complete the sentences.

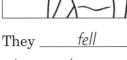
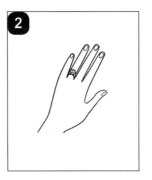

They _____*fell*_____   They _____   They _____   They _____ ____

_*in*_ _____*love*_____ .   _____ .   _____ .   _____ .

B Complete the conversation. Write the verbs in the past tense.

become	happen	meet	move	study	take

> **Interviewer:** When did you come to the United States?
>
> **Keysha:** In 1978, I went to college in New York. I _____*studied*_____
>   1
> English and accounting. I found a job. I was a waitress in a restaurant. I
>
> _____ my husband there. In 1980, I _____ the
>   2   3
> restaurant manager.
>
> **Interviewer:** What _____ after you got married?
>   4
> **Keysha:** We _____ the citizenship exam and became U.S.
>   5
> citizens. Then we _____ to Chicago. We started our own
>   6
> restaurant.

C Answer the questions. Use the information from Exercise B.

1. When did Keysha move to the United States? _*She immigrated in 1978.*_____

2. When did she become a manager? _____

3. When did she and her husband become citizens? _____

4. When did they start a business? _____

Name: _____

Lesson E *Writing*

A Complete the paragraph about Gloria Estefan.

married Emilio Estefan	Gloria was in a bus accident
son was born	to the United States in 1959

Gloria Estefan was born in 1957 in Havana, Cuba. She came
to the United States in 1959 . She started college in 1975. After
she graduated, she became a singer with the Miami Sound Machine. In
1978, she _____ . They have two children.
Her _____ in 1980. Her daughter was
born in 1994. In 1990, _____ . She broke
her back. She started to sing again in 1991. Her music is famous in many
countries around the world. She also wrote books for children in 2005
and 2006.

B Complete the time line. Use the information from Exercise A.

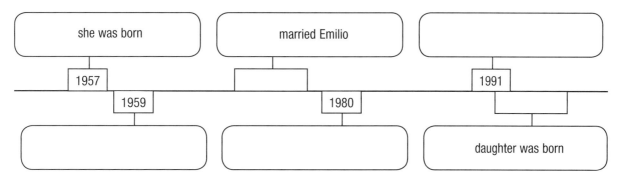

C Complete the sentences.

days	six	three	two	weeks	years

1. Today is June 23. I graduated on June 20. I graduated ___*three*___
   ___*days*___ ago.

2. It is 2008. I started my job in 2002. I started my job _____
   _____ ago.

3. It is September 21. I started English classes on September 7. I started
   classes _____ _____ ago.

Unit 6 Time

Name: _____

Lesson E *Writing*

A Complete the paragraph about Gloria Estefan.

Her son was born in 1980.	In 1990, Gloria was in a bus accident.
In 1978, she married Emilio Estefan.	She came to the United States in 1959.

Gloria Estefan was born in 1957 in Havana, Cuba. *She came to the United States in 1959.* She started college in 1975. After she graduated, she became a singer with the Miami Sound Machine. _____ They have two children. _____ Her daughter was born in 1994. _____ She broke her back. She started to sing again in 1991. Her music is famous in many countries around the world. She also wrote books for children in 2005 and 2006.

B Complete the time line. Use the information from Exercise A.

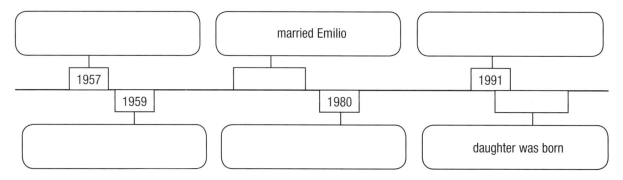

C Complete the sentences. Use some words more than once.

days	in	on	six	three	two	weeks	years

1. Today is June 23. I graduated __*on*__ June 20. I graduated __*three*__ __*days*__ ago.

2. It is 2008. I started my job _____ 2002. I started my job _____ _____ ago.

3. It is September 21. I started English classes _____ September 7. I started classes _____ _____ ago.

Lesson E *Writing*

A Complete the paragraph about Gloria Estefan.

Her son was born in 1980.	She also wrote books for children in 2005 and 2006.
In 1978, she married Emilio Estefan.	She came to the United States in 1959.
In 1990, Gloria was in a bus accident.	She started to sing again in 1991.

Gloria Estefan was born in 1957 in Havana, Cuba. *She came to the United States in 1959.* She started college in 1975. After she graduated, she became a singer with the Miami Sound Machine. _____ They have two children. _____ Her daughter was born in 1994. _____ She broke her back. _____

Her music is famous in many countries around the world.

_____

B Complete the time line. Use the information from Exercise A.

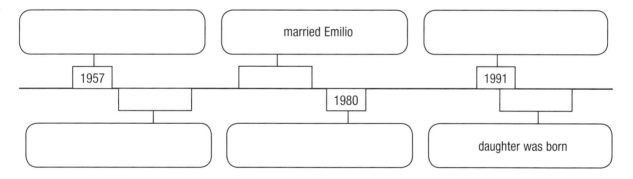

C Complete the sentences. Use the correct time phrases.

1. Today is June 23. I graduated _*on June 20*_ . I graduated three days ago.

2. It is 2008. I started my job _____ . I started my job six years ago.

3. It is September 21. I started English classes _____ . I started classes two weeks ago.

4. Today is Tuesday. I bought a car _____ ago. I bought the car on Saturday.

Lesson F *Another view*

A Look at the application for a marriage license. Circle the answers.

APPLICATION FOR A MARRIAGE LICENSE				
GROOM'S PERSONAL DATA				
First name Boris	**Middle** Arkady	**Last** Nazarov	**Birthdate** (Mo / Day / Yr) 05/15/1980	**Place of birth** Farley, Iowa
Street 123 Oak Street	**City** Farley	**State** Iowa	**Zip** 52046	**Phone** 563-555-3715
Father's name Fyodor Nazarov	**Place of birth** Moscow, Russia		**Mother's name** Paulina Dubowski	**Place of birth** Lublin, Poland
BRIDE'S PERSONAL DATA				
First name Marisa	**Middle** Louise	**Last** Brown	**Birthdate** (Mo / Day / Yr) 03/04/1981	**Place of birth** Ames, Iowa
Street 45 College Ave.	**City** Ames	**State** Iowa	**Zip** 50010	**Phone** 515-555-5653
Father's name Ralph Brown	**Place of birth** Chicago, Illinois		**Mother's name** Mary Novak	**Place of birth** Ames, Iowa
Ceremony date (Mo / Day / Yr) 04/07/2008	**Signature of groom** Boris A. Nazarov	**Date** 04/05/08	**Signature of bride** Marisa Brown	**Date** 04/05/08

1. When was the groom born?
   a. May 15, 1980
   b. March 4, 1981

2. When was the bride born?
   a. May 15, 1980
   b. March 4, 1981

3. Where was Boris's mother born?
   a. Lublin, Poland
   b. Moscow, Russia

4. Where was Marisa's father born?
   a. Ames, Iowa
   b. Chicago, Illinois

5. When was the wedding ceremony?
   a. April 7, 2008
   b. July 4, 2008

6. When did Boris and Marisa complete the marriage license application?
   a. April 5, 2008
   b. May 4, 2008

Unit 6 Time

Lesson F *Another view*

Name: _____

A Look at the application for a marriage license. Circle the answers.

APPLICATION FOR A MARRIAGE LICENSE				
GROOM'S PERSONAL DATA				
First name Boris	**Middle** Arkady	**Last** Nazarov	**Birthdate** (Mo / Day / Yr) 05/15/1980	**Place of birth** Farley, Iowa
Street 123 Oak Street	**City** Farley	**State** Iowa	**Zip** 52046	**Phone** 563-555-3715
Father's name Fyodor Nazarov	**Place of birth** Moscow, Russia	**Mother's name** Paulina Dubowski	**Place of birth** Lublin, Poland	
BRIDE'S PERSONAL DATA				
First name Marisa	**Middle** Louise	**Last** Brown	**Birthdate** (Mo / Day / Yr) 03/04/1981	**Place of birth** Ames, Iowa
Street 45 College Ave.	**City** Ames	**State** Iowa	**Zip** 50010	**Phone** 515-555-5653
Father's name Ralph Brown	**Place of birth** Chicago, Illinois	**Mother's name** Mary Novak	**Place of birth** Ames, Iowa	
Ceremony date (Mo / Day / Yr) 04/07/2008	**Signature of groom** Boris A. Nazarov	**Date** 04/05/08	**Signature of bride** Marisa Brown	**Date** 04/05/08

1. When was the groom born?
   a. March 4, 1981   c. April 3, 1981
   b. March 15, 1980   d. May 15, 1980

2. When was the bride born?
   a. March 4, 1981   c. April 3, 1981
   b. March 15, 1980   d. May 15, 1980

3. Where was Boris's mother born?
   a. Ames, Iowa   c. Lublin, Poland
   b. Chicago, Illinois d. Moscow, Russia

4. Where was Marisa's father born?
   a. Ames, Iowa   c. Lublin, Poland
   b. Chicago, Illinois d. Moscow, Russia

5. When was the wedding ceremony?
   a. April 7, 2008   c. May 7, 2008
   b. May 4, 2008   d. July 4, 2008

6. When did Boris and Marisa complete the marriage license application?
   a. April 5, 2008   c. May 4, 2008
   b. April 7, 2008   d. May 7, 2008

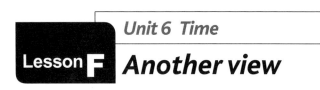

Name: _____

A Look at the application for a marriage license. Answer the questions.

APPLICATION FOR A MARRIAGE LICENSE				
GROOM'S PERSONAL DATA				
First name Boris	**Middle** Arkady	**Last** Nazarov	**Birthdate** (Mo / Day / Yr) 05/15/1980	**Place of birth** Farley, Iowa
Street 123 Oak Street	**City** Farley	**State** Iowa	**Zip** 52046	**Phone** 563-555-3715
Father's name Fyodor Nazarov	**Place of birth** Moscow, Russia		**Mother's name** Paulina Dubowski	**Place of birth** Lublin, Poland
BRIDE'S PERSONAL DATA				
First name Marisa	**Middle** Louise	**Last** Brown	**Birthdate** (Mo / Day / Yr) 03/04/1981	**Place of birth** Ames, Iowa
Street 45 College Ave.	**City** Ames	**State** Iowa	**Zip** 50010	**Phone** 515-555-5653
Father's name Ralph Brown	**Place of birth** Chicago, Illinois		**Mother's name** Mary Novak	**Place of birth** Ames, Iowa
Ceremony date (Mo / Day / Yr) 04/07/2008	**Signature of groom** Boris A. Nazarov	**Date** 04/05/08	**Signature of bride** Marisa Brown	**Date** 04/05/08

1. When was the groom born? _May 15, 1980_ _____

2. When was the bride born? _____

3. Where was Boris's mother born? _____

4. Where was Marisa's father born? _____

5. When was the wedding ceremony? _____

6. When did Boris and Marisa complete the marriage license application? _____

Lesson A *Get ready*

A Look at the picture. Write the words.

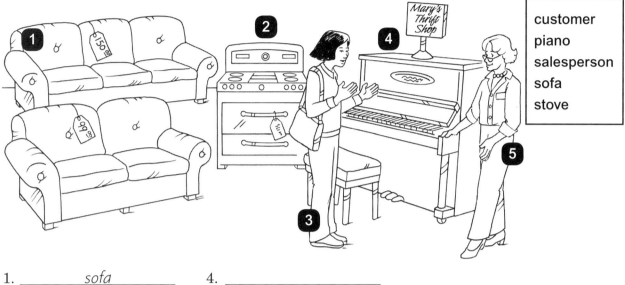

| customer |
| piano |
| salesperson |
| sofa |
| stove |

1. _____*sofa*_____   4. _____

2. _____   5. _____

3. _____

B Look at the picture in Exercise A. Complete the sentences.

| customer | furniture | price tag | salesperson |

1. The _____*customer*_____ wants to buy a piano.

2. The _____ is helping the customer.

3. The _____ _____ on the large sofa says $150.

4. Secondhand _____ is not new.

C Complete the information. Use the words from Exercise A.

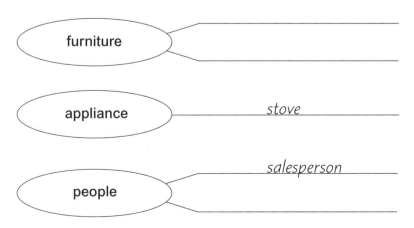

furniture _____

_____

appliance _____*stove*_____

_____

_____*salesperson*_____

people _____

Lesson A *Get ready*

Name: _____

A Look at the picture. Write the words.

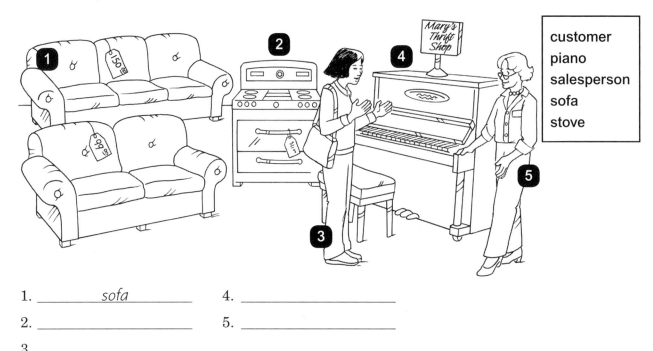

customer
piano
salesperson
sofa
stove

1. _____ *sofa* _____   4. _____
2. _____   5. _____
3. _____

B Look at the picture in Exercise A. Complete the sentences.

1. The c*ustomer* _____ wants to buy a piano.
2. The s_____ is helping the customer.
3. The p_____ t_____ on the large sofa says $150.
4. Secondhand f_____ is not new.

C Complete the information. Use the words from Exercise A and your own ideas.

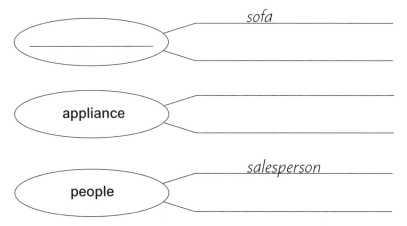

_____ *sofa* _____

_____

appliance

_____

_____

salesperson

people

_____

Lesson A *Get ready*

Name: _____

A Look at the picture. Write the words.

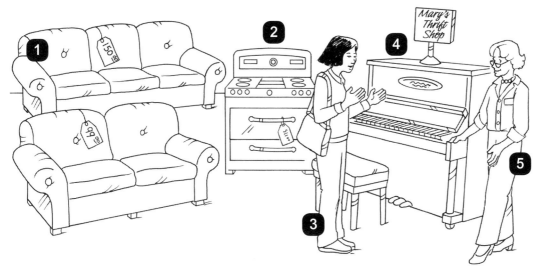

1. _____*sofa*_____   4. _____

2. _____   5. _____

3. _____

B Look at the picture in Exercise A. Complete the sentences.

1. The _____*customer*_____ wants to buy a piano.

2. The _____ is helping the customer.

3. The _____ _____ on the large sofa says $150.

4. Secondhand _____ is not new.

5. The large sofa is more _____ than the small sofa.

C Complete the information. Use the words from Exercise A and your own ideas.

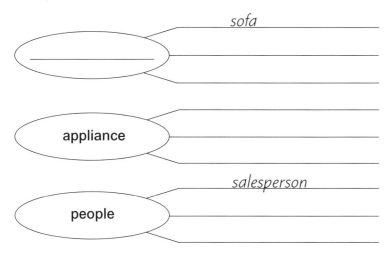

Name: _____

Lesson B *The brown sofa is bigger.*

A Write the comparative form.

1. cheap _*cheaper*_   3. expensive _____   5. small _____

2. big _____   4. good _____   6. comfortable _____

B Answer the questions. Write the letter of the picture.

1. **A** Which car is older?

   B Car _*a*_ .

2. **A** Which car is smaller?

   B Car ____ .

3. **A** Which sofa is more comfortable?

   B Sofa ____ .

4. **A** Which sofa is prettier?

   B Sofa ____ .

5. **A** Which table is cheaper?

   B Table ____ .

6. **A** Which table is longer?

   B Table ____ .

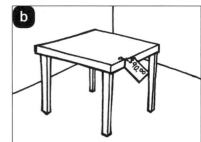

C Write a sentence that compares furniture in your home or classroom. Use comparatives.

My kitchen table is smaller than my dining table.

_____

Lesson B *The brown sofa is bigger.*

A Write the comparative form.

1. cheap ___*cheaper*___   5. small _____

2. big _____   6. comfortable _____

3. expensive _____   7. heavy _____

4. good _____   8. short _____

B Look at the pictures and the answers. Complete the questions.

1. **A** Which car is

   _____*older*_____ ?
   (older / newer)

   B Car a.

2. **A** Which car is

   _____ ?
   (larger / smaller)

   B Car b.

3. **A** Which sofa is

   _____ ?
   (more comfortable / smaller)

   B Sofa a.

4. **A** Which sofa is

   _____ ?
   (prettier / larger)

   B Sofa b.

5. **A** Which table is

   _____ ?
   (cheaper / more expensive)

   B Table b.

6. **A** Which table is

   _____ ?
   (longer / shorter)

   B Table a.

 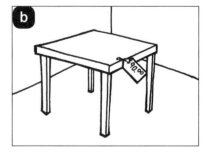

C Write two sentences that compare furniture in your home or classroom. Use comparatives.

My kitchen table is smaller than my dining table. _____

_____

Name: _____

Lesson B *The brown sofa is bigger.*

A Write the comparative form.

1. cheap __*cheaper*__

2. big _____

3. expensive _____

4. good _____

5. small _____

6. comfortable _____

7. heavy _____

8. short _____

9. pretty _____

10. long _____

11. tall _____

12. old _____

B Look at the pictures and the answers. Complete the questions. Use comparatives.

1. **A** Which car is

   _____*older*_____ ?
   (old / new)

   B Car a.

2. **A** Which car is

   _____ ?
   (large / small)

   B Car b.

3. **A** Which sofa is

   _____ ?
   (comfortable / small)

   B Sofa a.

4. **A** Which sofa is

   _____ ?
   (pretty / large)

   B Sofa b.

5. **A** Which table is

   _____ ?
   (cheap / expensive)

   B Table b.

6. **A** Which table is

   _____ ?
   (long / short)

   B Table a.

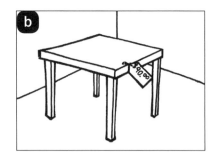

C Write three sentences that compare furniture in your home or classroom. Use comparatives.

My kitchen table is smaller than my dining table. _____

_____

_____

Name: _____

Lesson C *The yellow chair is the cheapest.* ☑ ■ ■

A Write the superlative form.

1. friendly _____*the friendliest*_____

2. nice _____

3. big _____

4. good _____

5. new _____

6. expensive _____

B Look at the chart. Answer the questions.

	$750 size: 26 inches	$500 size: 20 inches	$350 size: 15 inches
	$1,500 weight: 225 pounds	$750 weight: 150 pounds	$1,000 weight: 250 pounds

1. Which TV is the cheapest? _C_

2. Which TV is the most expensive? ____

3. Which TV is the largest? ____

4. Which refrigerator is the cheapest? ____

5. Which refrigerator is the most expensive? ____

6. Which refrigerator is the heaviest? ____

C Answer the questions about your neighborhood.

1. Which restaurant is the cheapest? _____

2. Which supermarket is the biggest? _____

3. Which clothing store is the best? _____

Lesson C *The yellow chair is the cheapest.*

A Write the superlative form.

1. friendly _____the friendliest_____

2. nice _____

3. big _____

4. good _____

5. new _____

6. expensive _____

7. cheap _____

8. heavy _____

B Look at the chart. Write questions and answers.

	$750 size: 26 inches	$500 size: 20 inches	$350 size: 15 inches
	$1,500 weight: 225 pounds	$750 weight: 150 pounds	$1,000 weight: 250 pounds

1. TV / Which / the / cheapest / is / ? _Which TV is the cheapest?_____ _C_

2. Which / is / TV / expensive / the / most / ? _____ ____

3. TV / the / Which / is / largest / ? _____ ____

4. refrigerator / Which / cheapest / the / is / ? _____ ____

5. the / expensive / most / Which / is / refrigerator / ? _____ ____

6. Which / the / heaviest / refrigerator / is / ? _____ ____

C Answer the questions about your neighborhood.

1. Which restaurant is the cheapest? _____

2. Which supermarket is the biggest? _____

3. Which clothing store is the best? _____

4. Which store is the most expensive? _____

Name: _____

Lesson C *The yellow chair is the cheapest.*

A Write the superlative form.

1. friendly _____*the friendliest*_____ 6. expensive _____
2. nice _____ 7. cheap _____
3. big _____ 8. heavy _____
4. good _____ 9. small _____
5. new _____ 10. beautiful _____

B Look at the chart. Write questions.

TV	$750 size: 26 inches	$500 size: 20 inches	$350 size: 15 inches
refrigerator	$1,500 weight: 225 pounds	$750 weight: 150 pounds	$1,000 weight: 250 pounds

1. (TV / cheapest) _*Which TV is the cheapest?*_____ _C_
2. (TV / the most expensive) _____ ____
3. (TV / the largest) _____ ____
4. (refrigerator / the cheapest) _____ ____
5. (refrigerator / the most expensive) _____ ____
6. (refrigerator / the heaviest) _____ ____

C Answer the questions about your neighborhood.

1. Which restaurant is the cheapest? _____
2. Which supermarket is the biggest? _____
3. Which clothing store is the best? _____
4. Which store is the most expensive? _____
5. Which store has the friendliest salespeople? _____

A Cross out the word that does not belong in each group.

1. cheapest   longest   ~~prettier~~

2. smallest   bigger   lower

3. end table   china cabinet   coffee table

4. mirror   sofa bed   salesperson

B Read the article. Match the questions with the answers.

What's the best thing you ever bought?

"The best thing I ever bought was a new entertainment center. It's bigger than my old entertainment center. Now I want to watch TV and listen to music all day."

Christine Wilson
Houston, TX

"The best thing I ever bought was a new recliner. It's more comfortable than my old recliner. Now I can relax after work."

Helen Jones
Columbus, OH

1. What did Christine buy?
2. Why did Christine buy it?
3. What did Helen buy?
4. Why did Helen buy it?
5. What does Christine want to do now?
6. What can Helen do now?

a. Helen can relax.
b. Christine bought an entertainment center.
c. Christine wants to watch TV all day.
d. Helen bought a recliner.
e. It's more comfortable.
f. It's bigger.

C Complete the sentences.

1. The best thing I ever bought was _____ .
2. The most expensive thing I ever bought was _____ .
3. The most useful thing I ever bought was _____ .

Lesson D *Reading*

Name: _____

A Cross out the word that does not belong in each group.

1. cheapest   longest   ~~prettier~~   heaviest
2. smallest   bigger   lower   longer
3. end table   china cabinet   coffee table   dining table
4. mirror   sofa bed   salesperson   chair

B Read the article. Answer the questions.

What's the best thing you ever bought?

"The best thing I ever bought was a new entertainment center. It's bigger than my old entertainment center. Now I want to watch TV and listen to music all day."

Christine Wilson
Houston, TX

"The best thing I ever bought was a new recliner. It's more comfortable than my old recliner. Now I can relax after work."

Helen Jones
Columbus, OH

1. What did Christine buy? *Christine bought an entertainment center.* _____
2. Why did Christine buy it? _____
3. What did Helen buy? _____
4. Why did Helen buy it? _____
5. What does Christine want to do now? _____
6. What can Helen do now? _____

C Answer the questions.

1. What is the best thing you ever bought? _____
2. What is the most expensive thing you ever bought? _____
3. What is the most useful thing you ever bought? _____

Name: _____

Lesson D Reading

A Cross out the word that does not belong in each group.

1.	cheapest	longest	~~prettier~~	heaviest	best
2.	smallest	bigger	nicer	lower	older
3.	end table	china cabinet	coffee table	dining table	kitchen table
4.	mirror	sofa bed	salesperson	chair	recliner

B Read the article. Read the answers. Write questions.

What's the best thing you ever bought?

"The best thing I ever bought was a new entertainment center. It's bigger than my old entertainment center. Now I want to watch TV and listen to music all day."

Christine Wilson
Houston, TX

"The best thing I ever bought was a new recliner. It's more comfortable than my old recliner. Now I can relax after work."

Helen Jones
Columbus, OH

1. What _did Christine buy_____ ? Christine bought an entertainment center.

2. Why _____ ? It's bigger.

3. What _____ ? Helen bought a recliner.

4. Why _____ ? It's more comfortable.

5. What _____ ? Christine wants to watch TV all day.

6. What _____ ? Helen can relax after work now.

C Answer the questions.

1. What is the best thing you ever bought? _____

2. What is the most expensive thing you ever bought? _____

3. What is the most useful thing you ever bought? _____

4. What is the most comfortable thing you ever bought? _____

Name: _____

Lesson E Writing

A Read about Tina's gift. Match the questions with the answers.

> The best gift I ever received was a bicycle. My dad gave it to me for my tenth birthday. It was a long time ago! It came from the bicycle store near our home. It was the best gift because I really needed it. I rode it to school every day for three years. Then I gave it to my younger brother for his birthday.

1. What is the best gift Tina ever received?

2. Who gave it to her?

3. Why did she receive it?

4. Where did the gift come from?

5. When did she receive this gift?

6. Why was it the best gift?

7. What happened to the gift?

a. It was for her tenth birthday.

b. She really needed it.

c. She gave it to her brother.

d. The best gift she ever received was a bicycle.

e. It came from the bicycle store near her home.

f. Her father gave it to her.

g. It was a long time ago.

B Think of the best gift you ever gave to a friend or a family member. Answer the questions.

1. What was the gift? _____

2. Who was it for? _____

3. Why did you give the gift? _____

4. Why was it the best gift? _____

C Write a paragraph about the best gift you ever gave to a friend or a family member. Use the information from Exercise B.

The best gift I ever gave to a friend was . . . _____

_____

_____

_____

_____

_____

Lesson E *Writing*

Name: _____

A Read about Tina's gift. Answer the questions.

> The best gift I ever received was a bicycle. My dad gave it to me for my tenth birthday. It was a long time ago! It came from the bicycle store near our home. It was the best gift because I really needed it. I rode it to school every day for three years. Then I gave it to my younger brother for his birthday.

1. What is the best gift Tina ever received? *The best gift she ever received was a bicycle.*

2. Who gave it to her? _____

3. Why did she receive it? _____

4. Where did the gift come from? _____

5. When did she receive this gift? _____

6. Why was it the best gift? _____

7. What happened to the gift? _____

B Think of the best gift you ever gave to a friend or a family member. Answer the questions.

1. What was the gift? _____

2. Who was it for? _____

3. Why did you give the gift? _____

4. Where did the gift come from? _____

5. When did you give the gift? _____

6. Why was it the best gift? _____

C Write a paragraph about the best gift you ever gave to a friend or a family member. Use the information from Exercise B.

_____

_____

_____

_____

_____

Name: _____

Lesson E *Writing*

A Read about Tina's gift. Read the answers. Write the questions.

> *The best gift I ever received was a bicycle. My dad gave it to me for my tenth birthday. It was a long time ago! It came from the bicycle store near our home. It was the best gift because I really needed it. I rode it to school every day for three years. Then I gave it to my younger brother for his birthday.*

1. What *is the best gift Tina ever received* ? The best gift she ever received was a bicycle.
2. Who _____ ? Her father gave it to her.
3. Why _____ ? It was for her tenth birthday.
4. Where _____ ? It came from the bicycle store near her home.
5. When _____ ? It was a long time ago.
6. Why _____ ? She really needed it.
7. What _____ ? She gave it to her brother.

B Think of the best gift you ever gave to a friend or a family member. Answer the questions.

1. What was the gift? _____
2. Who was it for? _____
3. Why did you give the gift? _____
4. Where did the gift come from? _____
5. When did you give the gift? _____
6. Why was it the best gift? _____

C Write a paragraph about the best gift you ever gave to a friend or a family member. Use the information from Exercise B.

_____

_____

_____

_____

_____

_____

Lesson F *Another view*

Name:

A Look at the sales receipt. Circle the answers.

	Sales Receipt	
	Sales Receipt	
	Bob's Home Appliances and Furniture	
	32 Greenview Road	
	El Paso, TX 79925	

Salesperson: Bob Johnson Date: 05 / 01 / 08
Customer: Juan Ramos Phone: 937-555-5788
Address: 4141 Dayton Road
City: El Paso State: TX Zip code: 79925

Quantity	Description	Price
1	refrigerator	$900.00
1	end table	$310.00
1	stove	$500.00
1	china cabinet	$250.00
	Subtotal	$1,960.00
	Sales tax 8.25%	$161.70
	Total	$2,121.70

No refunds or exchanges after 90 days.

1. What is the cheapest item?
   a. the china cabinet *(circled)*
   b. the end table
   c. the stove

2. What is the most expensive item?
   a. the end table
   b. the refrigerator
   c. the stove

3. Which items are appliances?
   a. the refrigerator and the end table
   b. the refrigerator and the stove
   c. the stove and the china cabinet

4. When can a customer *not* exchange an item?
   a. after 7 days
   b. after 30 days
   c. after 90 days

5. What is the total before tax?
   a. $161.70
   b. $1,960.00
   c. $2,121.70

6. What is the total after tax?
   a. $161.70
   b. $1,960.00
   c. $2,121.70

B Look at the receipt from Exercise A. Answer the questions.

1. Who is the customer? _____

2. Who is the salesperson? _____

3. What percent is the sales tax? _____

Name: _____

Lesson F *Another view*

A Look at the sales receipt. Correct the false information in the sentences.

Sales Receipt		
Bob's Home Appliances and Furniture		
32 Greenview Road		
El Paso, TX 79925		

Salesperson: Bob Johnson

Customer: Juan Ramos

Address: 4141 Dayton Road

City: El Paso State: TX

Date: 05 / 01 / 08

Phone: 937-555-5788

Zip code: 79925

Quantity	Description	Price
1	refrigerator	$900.00
1	end table	$310.00
1	stove	$500.00
1	china cabinet	$250.00
	Subtotal	$1,960.00
	Sales tax 8.25%	$161.70
	Total	$2,121.70

No refunds or exchanges after 90 days.

1. The cheapest item is <u>the end table</u>. *the china cabinet*

2. The most expensive item is <u>the stove</u>. _____

3. The <u>china cabinet</u> and the <u>stove</u> are appliances. _____

4. A customer cannot exchange an item after <u>100</u> days. _____

5. The total before tax is <u>$2,121.70</u>. _____

6. The total after tax is <u>$161.70</u>. _____

B Look at the receipt from Exercise A. Answer the questions.

1. Who is the customer? _____

2. Who is the salesperson? _____

3. What percent is the sales tax? _____

4. Where is the store? _____

Name: _____

Lesson F Another view

A Look at the sales receipt. Answer the questions.

	Sales Receipt	
	Bob's Home Appliances and Furniture	
	32 Greenview Road	
	El Paso, TX 79925	

Salesperson: Bob Johnson   Date: 05 / 01 / 08
Customer: Juan Ramos   Phone: 937-555-5788
Address: 4141 Dayton Road
City: El Paso   State: TX   Zip code: 79925

Quantity	Description	Price
1	refrigerator	$900.00
1	end table	$310.00
1	stove	$500.00
1	china cabinet	$250.00
	Subtotal	$1,960.00
	Sales tax 8.25%	$161.70
	Total	**$2,121.70**

No refunds or exchanges after 90 days.

1. What is the cheapest item? _the china cabinet_

2. What is the most expensive item? _____

3. Which items are appliances? _____

4. When can a customer *not* exchange an item? _____

5. What is the total before tax? _____

6. What is the total after tax? _____

B Look at the receipt from Exercise A. Answer the questions.

1. Who is the customer? _____

2. Who is the salesperson? _____

3. What percent is the sales tax? _____

4. Where is the store? _____

5. What is the customer's address? _____

Name: _____

Lesson A *Get ready*

A Find the words.

| co-worker | linens | patient | walker |
| lab | orderly | supplies | wheelchair |

t	r	e	w	y	u	i	k	j	p	c	d	x
l	o	h	s	p	l	a	t	l	a	o	f	r
i	f	l	u	n	v	r	o	c	t	w	t	y
n	a	i	p	l	a	t	p	h	i	o	e	a
e	w	e	p	u	c	o	r	d	e	r	l	y
n	e	f	l	a	b	e	r	s	n	k	c	l
s	b	r	i	s	x	b	i	g	t	e	v	m
c	w	h	e	e	l	c	h	a	i	r	b	n
r	b	o	s	r	o	d	w	a	l	k	e	r

B Look at the pictures. Complete the sentences.

| co-worker | linens | orderly | patient | supplies | walker | wheelchair |

1. The _____*patient*_____ has a broken leg and needs a _____*wheelchair*_____ .

2. The _____ is delivering _____ .

3. She is using a _____ .

4. He is giving some medical _____ to his _____ .

A Find the words.

co-worker	linens	patient	walker
lab	orderly	supplies	wheelchair

t	r	e	w	y	u	i	k	j	p	c	d	x
l	o	h	s	p	l	a	t	l	a	o	f	r
i	f	l	u	n	v	r	o	c	t	w	t	y
n	a	i	p	l	a	t	p	h	i	o	e	a
e	w	e	p	u	c	o	r	d	e	r	l	y
n	e	f	l	a	b	e	r	s	n	k	c	l
s	b	r	i	s	x	b	i	g	t	e	v	m
c	w	h	e	e	l	c	h	a	i	r	b	n
r	b	o	s	r	o	d	w	a	l	k	e	r

B Look at the pictures. Complete the sentences. Use words from Exercise A.

1. The p*atient*_____ has a broken leg and needs a w *heelchair*_____ .

2. The o_____ is delivering l_____ .

3. She is using a w_____ .

4. He is giving some medical s_____ to his c_____ .

Lesson A *Get ready*

Name: _____

A Find eight words from Lesson A.

t	r	e	w	y	u	i	k	j	p	c	d	x
l	o	h	s	p	l	a	t	l	a	o	f	r
i	f	l	u	n	v	r	o	c	t	w	t	y
n	a	i	p	l	a	t	p	h	i	o	e	a
e	w	e	p	u	c	o	r	d	e	r	l	y
n	e	f	l	a	b	e	r	s	n	k	c	l
s	b	r	i	s	x	b	i	g	t	e	v	m
c	w	h	e	e	l	c	h	a	i	r	b	n
r	b	o	s	r	o	d	w	a	l	k	e	r

B Look at the pictures. Complete the sentences. Use words from Exercise A.

1. The _____*patient*_____ has a broken leg and needs a ____*wheelchair*____ .

2. The _____ is delivering _____ .

3. She is using a _____ .

4. He is giving some medical _____ to his _____ .

Lesson B *Where did you go last night?*

A Alan is an orderly. What did he do yesterday? Circle the answers.

1. He ___ breakfast.   a. met   (b. ate)   c. helped

2. He ___ the beds.   a. made   b. studied   c. took

3. He ___ the furniture.   a. helped   b. cleaned   c. met

4. He ___ X-rays.   a. cleaned   b. started   c. delivered

5. He ___ patients.   a. made   b. met   c. started

B Read the information in the chart. Answer the questions.

Angela		Inez and Martin	
10:00 a.m.	went to a meeting	8:30 a.m.	took the linens to the eighth floor
10:30 a.m.	picked up X-rays	9:00 a.m.	prepared rooms on the sixth floor
11:00 a.m.	made the beds on the fourth floor	10:30 a.m.	cleaned the furniture

1. What did Angela do at 10:00?

   She went to a meeting.

2. What did Inez and Martin do at 8:30?

   _____

3. What did Inez and Martin do at 9:00?

   _____

4. What did Angela do at 10:30?

   _____

C What did you do last Saturday? Where did you go? Complete the chart.

Time	What did you do?	Where did you go?

D Complete the sentence. Use your information from Exercise C.

Last Saturday, I _____ .

Name: _____

Lesson B *Where did you go last night?*

A Alan is an orderly. What did he do yesterday? Complete the sentences.

ate	cleaned	delivered	made	met

1. He _____*ate*_____ breakfast.   4. He _____ X-rays.

2. He _____ the beds.   5. He _____ patients.

3. He _____ the furniture.

B Read the information in the chart. Write questions and answers.

Angela		Inez and Martin	
10:00 a.m.	*went to a meeting*	8:30 a.m.	*took the linens to the eighth floor*
10:30 a.m.	*picked up X-rays*	9:00 a.m.	*prepared rooms on the sixth floor*
11:00 a.m.	*made the beds on the fourth floor*	10:30 a.m.	*cleaned the furniture*

1. 10:00 / do / did / at / Angela / What _*What did Angela do at 10:00*_ ?

   *She went to a meeting.*

2. 8:30 / at / Inez and Martin / did / do / What _____ ?

   _____

3. Inez and Martin / did / do / 9:00 / at / What _____ ?

   _____

4. Angela / 10:30 / did / at / do / What _____ ?

   _____

C What did you do last Saturday? Where did you go? Complete the chart.

Time	What did you do?	Where did you go?

D Write two sentences. Use your information from Exercise C.

1. _____

2. _____

Name: _____

Lesson B *Where did you go last night?* ■ ■ ☑

A Alan is an orderly. What did he do yesterday? Complete the sentences.
Use the past tense.

clean	deliver	eat	make	meet

1. He _____*ate*_____ breakfast.

2. He _____ the beds.

3. He _____ the furniture.

4. He _____ X-rays.

5. He _____ patients.

B Read the information in the chart. Write questions with *What* and answers.

	Angela		Inez and Martin
10:00 a.m.	*went to a meeting*	8:30 a.m.	*took the linens to the eighth floor*
10:30 a.m.	*picked up X-rays*	9:00 a.m.	*prepared rooms on the sixth floor*
11:00 a.m.	*made the beds on the fourth floor*	10:30 a.m.	*cleaned the furniture*

1. (Angela) _*What did Angela do*_____ at 10:00?

   _*She went to a meeting.*_____

2. (Inez and Martin) _____ at 8:30?

   _____

3. (Inez and Martin) _____ at 9:00?

   _____

4. (Angela) _____ at 10:30?

   _____

C What did you do last Saturday? Where did you go? Complete the chart.

Time	What did you do?	Where did you go?

D Write two sentences. Use your information from Exercise C.

1. _____

2. _____

Lesson **C** *I work on Saturdays and Sundays.*

A Combine the sentences.

1. Sometimes Miguel takes the bus to work. Sometimes he rides his bike. (or)

   Miguel takes the bus to work or rides his bike _____

2. He goes to meetings. He doesn't take notes. (but)

   _____

3. He delivers mail. He also makes copies. (and)

   _____

4. He answers calls. He doesn't take messages. (but)

   _____

5. Sometimes he eats lunch in the cafeteria. Sometimes he eats at his desk. (or)

   _____

6. Sometimes he goes home after work. Sometimes he visits a friend. (or)

   _____

B Check (✓) the things you like to do.

- ☐ check e-mail
- ☐ write letters
- ☐ answer calls
- ☐ take messages
- ☐ eat in a restaurant
- ☐ eat outside

C Write two sentences about the information in Exercise B. Use *and*, *or*, or *but*.

I like to check e-mail, but I don't like to write letters. _____

1. _____

2. _____

Name: _____

Lesson C *I work on Saturdays and Sundays.*

A Combine the sentences. Use *and*, *or*, or *but*.

1. Sometimes Miguel takes the bus to work. Sometimes he rides his bike.

   Miguel takes the bus to work or rides his bike. _____

2. He goes to meetings. He doesn't take notes.

   _____

3. He delivers mail. He also makes copies.

   _____

4. He answers calls. He doesn't take messages.

   _____

5. Sometimes he eats lunch in the cafeteria. Sometimes he eats at his desk.

   _____

6. Sometimes he goes home after work. Sometimes he visits a friend.

   _____

B Check (✓) the things you like to do.

☐ **check e-mail**
☐ **write letters**
☐ **answer calls**
☐ **take messages**
☐ **eat in a restaurant**
☐ **eat outside**
☐ **go to work**
☐ **go to school**

C Write three sentences about the information in Exercise B. Use *and*, *or*, or *but*.

I like to check e-mail, but I don't like to write letters. _____

1. _____

2. _____

3. _____

Lesson C *I work on Saturdays and Sundays.* ■ ■ ☑

A Complete the sentences. Use *and*, *or*, or *but*.

doesn't take messages	makes copies
doesn't take notes	rides his bike
eats at his desk	visits a friend

1. Miguel takes the bus to work *or rides his bike* _____ .

2. He goes to meetings _____ .

3. He delivers mail _____ .

4. He answers calls _____ .

5. He eats lunch in the cafeteria _____ .

6. He goes home after work _____ .

B Check (✓) the things you like to do.

☐ check e-mail
☐ write letters
☐ answer calls
☐ take messages
☐ eat in a restaurant
☐ eat outside
☐ go to work
☐ go to school
☐ go to meetings
☐ take notes

C Write four sentences about the information in Exercise B. Use *and*, *or*, or *but*.

I like to check e-mail, but I don't like to write letters. _____

1. _____

2. _____

3. _____

4. _____

Lesson **D** *Reading*

A Read the clues. Complete the puzzle.

assistant	cashier	cook	housewife	mechanic	orderly

```
            ¹h
          ²o _ _ _ _ _
            u
  ³ s _ _ _ _ _ _ _
            e
            w    ⁴
            i
            f
  ⁵ e _ _ _ _ _  ⁶
```

Down
1. This person takes care of a family.
4. This person handles money.
6. This person prepares food.

Across
2. This person helps the nurses.
3. This person helps the dentist.
5. This person repairs cars.

B Read the letter of recommendation. Match the questions with the answers.

> January 23, 2008
>
> Dear Dr. Jackson,
>
>   I am happy to write this letter of recommendation for Fernanda Garcia. Fernanda started working at South Town Dentists as a full-time dental assistant in 2005. She takes good care of patients. She is an excellent worker, and her co-workers like her very much. She is leaving because she needs to find a job closer to her home.
>
> Sincerely,
>
> *Denise Stephens*
> Denise Stephens

1. Who wrote the letter?   a. She wants to work closer to home.

2. What is Fernanda's job?   b. She started in 2005.

3. When did she start?   c. Denise Stephens wrote the letter.

4. Why is she leaving?   d. She is a dental assistant.

Lesson D *Reading*

A Read the clues. Complete the puzzle.

	¹h						
	²o						
	u						
³a	s						
	e						
	w	⁴c					
	i						
	f						
⁵m	e				⁶c		

Down

1. A ___ takes care of a family.
4. A ___ handles money.
6. A ___ prepares food.

Across

2. An ___ helps the nurses.
3. An ___ helps the dentist.
5. A ___ repairs cars.

B Read the letter of recommendation. Answer the questions.

January 23, 2008

Dear Dr. Jackson,

   I am happy to write this letter of recommendation for Fernanda Garcia. Fernanda started working at South Town Dentists as a full-time dental assistant in 2005. She takes good care of patients. She is an excellent worker, and her co-workers like her very much. She is leaving because she needs to find a job closer to her home.

Sincerely,

Denise Stephens

Denise Stephens

1. Who wrote the letter? *Denise Stephens wrote the letter.* _____
2. What is Fernanda's job? _____
3. When did she start? _____
4. Why is she leaving? _____

Lesson D *Reading*

Name: _____

A Read the clues. Complete the puzzle.

	¹h						
	²o						
	u						
³	s						
	e						
	w	⁴					
	i						
	f						
⁵	e				⁶		

Down

1. This person takes care of a family.
4. This person handles money.
6. This person prepares food.

Across

2. This person helps the nurses.
3. This person helps the dentist.
5. This person repairs cars.

B Read the letter of recommendation and the answers. Complete the questions.

> January 23, 2008
>
> Dear Dr. Jackson,
>
>   I am happy to write this letter of recommendation for Fernanda Garcia. Fernanda started working at South Town Dentists as a full-time dental assistant in 2005. She takes good care of patients. She is an excellent worker, and her co-workers like her very much. She is leaving because she needs to find a job closer to her home.
>
> Sincerely,
>
> *Denise Stephens*
> Denise Stephens

1. Who *wrote the letter* _____? Denise Stephens wrote the letter.

2. What _____? She is a dental assistant.

3. When _____? She started in 2005.

4. Why _____? She wants to work closer to home.

Unit 8 Work

Lesson E *Writing*

Name: _____

A Look at the chart. Match the questions with the answers.

Paolo Fonseca 4433 Hill Street San Francisco, CA 94114			
Job	*Place*	*Years*	*Job duties*
Waiter	Mom's Kitchen	2005–present	Serve food, talk to customers
Cook	Hot Tamale Restaurant	2004–2005	Prepared food
Busboy	Tito's Cantina	2002–2003	Cleared tables

1. Where does Paolo work?

2. What was his job in 2004?

3. What are his job duties now?

4. What were his job duties in 2002?

5. Where did he work in 2003?

a. He serves food and talks to customers.

b. He worked at Tito's Cantina.

c. He was a cook.

d. He works at Mom's Kitchen.

e. He cleared tables.

B Read Chisako's employment history. Complete the conversation.

> Chisako is an orderly at South City Hospital. She started in 2005. She has many job duties. She helps the nurses and the doctors. She prepares rooms for the patients. She meets patients in the reception area. She also picks up and delivers X-rays and medical supplies.
>
> From 2003 to 2005, Chisako worked at Lucky's Supermarket. She was a cashier. She handled money and helped customers.

Interviewer What is your job?

   Chisako *I am an orderly.* _____

Interviewer Where do you work?

   Chisako _____

Interviewer What are your duties?

   Chisako _____

         _____

Interviewer What job did you have before?

   Chisako _____

Name: _____

Lesson E Writing

A Look at the chart. Correct the false information in the sentences.

Paolo Fonseca			
4433 Hill Street San Francisco, CA 94114			
Job	*Place*	*Years*	*Job duties*
Waiter	Mom's Kitchen	2005–present	Serve food, talk to customers
Cook	Hot Tamale Restaurant	2004–2005	Prepared food
Busboy	Tito's Cantina	2002–2003	Cleared tables

1. Paolo works at <u>Tito's Cantina</u>. *Paolo works at Mom's Kitchen.*

2. He was <u>a busboy</u> in 2004. _____

3. He <u>clears tables</u> now. _____

4. He <u>prepared food</u> in 2002. _____

5. He worked at <u>Mom's Kitchen</u> in 2003. _____

B Read Chisako's employment history. Complete the conversation.

> Chisako is an orderly at South City Hospital. She started in 2005. She has many job duties. She helps the nurses and the doctors. She prepares rooms for the patients. She meets patients in the reception area. She also picks up and delivers X-rays and medical supplies.
>
> From 2003 to 2005, Chisako worked at Lucky's Supermarket. She was a cashier. She handled money and helped customers.

Interviewer What is your job?

Chisako *I am an orderly.* _____

Interviewer Where do you work?

Chisako _____

Interviewer What are your duties?

Chisako _____

_____

Interviewer What job did you have before?

Chisako _____

Interviewer Where did you work?

Chisako _____

Lesson E *Writing*

A Look at the chart. Answer the questions.

Paolo Fonseca 4433 Hill Street San Francisco, CA 94114			
Job	*Place*	*Years*	*Job duties*
Waiter	Mom's Kitchen	2005–present	Serve food, talk to customers
Cook	Hot Tamale Restaurant	2004–2005	Prepared food
Busboy	Tito's Cantina	2002–2003	Cleared tables

1. Where does Paolo work? *Paolo works at Mom's Kitchen.* _____

2. What was his job in 2004? _____

3. What are his job duties now? _____

4. What were his job duties in 2002? _____

5. Where did he work in 2003? _____

B Read Chisako's employment history. Complete the conversation.

> Chisako is an orderly at South City Hospital. She started in 2005. She has many job duties. She helps the nurses and the doctors. She prepares rooms for the patients. She meets patients in the reception area. She also picks up and delivers X-rays and medical supplies.
>
> From 2003 to 2005, Chisako worked at Lucky's Supermarket. She was a cashier. She handled money and helped customers.

Interviewer What is your job?

    Chisako *I am an orderly.* _____

Interviewer Where do you work?

    Chisako _____

Interviewer What are your duties?

    Chisako _____

    _____

Interviewer What job did you have before?

    Chisako _____

Interviewer Where did you work?

    Chisako _____

Name: _____

Lesson F **Another view**

A Look at the time sheet. Circle the answers.

Big Burger Bar – Weekly Time Sheet						
Employee: Ellen Fidorka				Social Security Number: 000-99-1234		
Rate: $8.50 / hour						
Day	Date	Time in	Time out	Time in	Time out	Hours
Monday	5/16	4:00 p.m.	7:00 p.m.	7:30 p.m.	10:30 p.m.	6
Tuesday	5/17	4:30 p.m.	7:30 p.m.	8:00 p.m.	11:00 p.m.	6
Wednesday	5/18	4:00 p.m.	7:00 p.m.	7:30 p.m.	10:30 p.m.	6
Thursday	5/19	4:00 p.m.	7:00 p.m.	7:30 p.m.	10:30 p.m.	6
Friday	5/20	5:30 p.m.	9:30 p.m.	10:00 p.m.	12:30 a.m.	6.5
Total Hours						

1. What is Ellen's hourly rate?

   a. 4:00–10:30   b. 6 hours   c. $8.50

2. When did she start work on Thursday?

   a. 4:00 p.m.   b. 4:30 p.m.   c. 5:30 p.m.

3. When did she leave work on Tuesday?

   a. 10:30 p.m.   b. 11:00 p.m.   c. 12:30 a.m.

4. What day did she start work at 5:30 p.m.?

   a. Tuesday   b. Thursday   c. Friday

5. How long is her dinner break?

   a. one hour   b. 30 minutes   c. 15 minutes

6. What is the total number of hours she worked this week?

   a. 30   b. 30.5   c. 35

B Complete the conversations.

1. **A** These books are very heavy!

   B Can I give you a _____ *hand* _____ ?
       (help / hand)

2. **A** What are you going to study next year?

   B I don't know. I can't make _____ my mind.
       (up / out)

3. **A** Did you get a lot of letters today?

   B No, it was a lot of _____ mail.
       (junk / trash)

4. **A** Was the test difficult?

   B No, it was a piece of _____ .
       (work / cake)

Name: _____

Lesson F Another view

A Look at the time sheet. Answer the questions.

Big Burger Bar – Weekly Time Sheet						
Employee: Ellen Fidorka				**Social Security Number:** 000-99-1234		
Rate: $8.50 / hour						
Day	**Date**	**Time in**	**Time out**	**Time in**	**Time out**	**Hours**
Monday	5/16	4:00 p.m.	7:00 p.m.	7:30 p.m.	10:30 p.m.	6
Tuesday	5/17	4:30 p.m.	7:30 p.m.	8:00 p.m.	11:00 p.m.	6
Wednesday	5/18	4:00 p.m.	7:00 p.m.	7:30 p.m.	10:30 p.m.	6
Thursday	5/19	4:00 p.m.	7:00 p.m.	7:30 p.m.	10:30 p.m.	6
Friday	5/20	5:30 p.m.	9:30 p.m.	10:00 p.m.	12:30 a.m.	6.5
Total Hours						

1. What is Ellen's hourly rate? *$8.50* _____

2. When did she start work on Thursday? _____

3. When did she leave work on Tuesday? _____

4. What day did she start work at 5:30 p.m.? _____

5. How long is her dinner break? _____

6. What is the total number of hours she worked this week? _____

B Complete the conversations.

a hand   junk mail   make up my mind   a piece of cake

1. **A** These books are very heavy!

   B Can I give you *a hand* _____ ?

2. **A** What are you going to study next year?

   B I don't know. I can't _____ .

3. **A** Did you get a lot of letters today?

   B No, it was a lot of _____ .

4. **A** Was the test difficult?

   B No, it was _____ .

Lesson F *Another view*

Name: _____

A Look at the time sheet. Complete the questions.

Big Burger Bar – Weekly Time Sheet						
Employee: Ellen Fidorka				**Social Security Number:** 000-99-1234		
Rate: $8.50 / hour						
Day	**Date**	**Time in**	**Time out**	**Time in**	**Time out**	**Hours**
Monday	5/16	4:00 p.m.	7:00 p.m.	7:30 p.m.	10:30 p.m.	6
Tuesday	5/17	4:30 p.m.	7:30 p.m.	8:00 p.m.	11:00 p.m.	6
Wednesday	5/18	4:00 p.m.	7:00 p.m.	7:30 p.m.	10:30 p.m.	6
Thursday	5/19	4:00 p.m.	7:00 p.m.	7:30 p.m.	10:30 p.m.	6
Friday	5/20	5:30 p.m.	9:30 p.m.	10:00 p.m.	12:30 a.m.	6.5
Total Hours						

1. What *is Ellen's hourly rate* ? $8.50

2. When did she _____ on Thursday?   4:00 p.m.

3. When did she _____ on Tuesday?   11:00 p.m.

4. What day did she _____ at 5:30 p.m.?   Friday

5. How _____ dinner break?   30 minutes

6. What is the total _____ she worked this week?   30.5

B Rewrite each sentence. Use idioms.

a hand   junk mail   make up my mind   a piece of cake

1. **A** These books are very heavy!

   B Can I give you <u>some help</u>? *Can I give you a hand?* _____

2. **A** What are you going to study next year?

   B I don't know. I can't <u>decide</u>. _____

3. **A** Did you get a lot of letters today?

   B No, it was a lot of <u>advertisements</u>. _____

4. **A** Was the test difficult?

   B No, it was <u>easy</u>. _____

Lesson A *Get ready* ☑ ■ ■

A Look at the pictures. Write the words.

| dishwasher | garbage | lightbulb | washing machine |

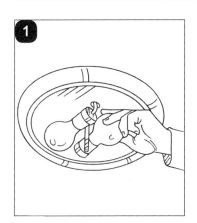

1. _____*lightbulb*_____   3. _____

2. _____   4. _____

B Number the sentences in the correct order.

__1__ Mrs. Chan's washing machine was leaking.

_____ The neighbor called the building manager.

_____ The building manager called a plumber.

_____ Mrs. Chan's neighbor saw water under the door.

_____ The plumber came and fixed the leak.

Lesson A *Get ready*

A Look at the pictures. Write the words.

| dishwasher | garbage | lightbulb | washing machine |

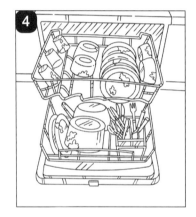

1. _____*lightbulb*_____   3. _____

2. _____   4. _____

B Number the sentences in the correct order.

__1__ Mrs. Chan's washing machine was leaking.

_____ The neighbor called the building manager.

_____ The building manager called a plumber.

_____ Mrs. Chan thanked her neighbor the next day.

_____ Mrs. Chan's neighbor saw water under the door.

_____ The plumber came and fixed the leak.

Lesson A Get ready

A Look at the pictures. Write the words.

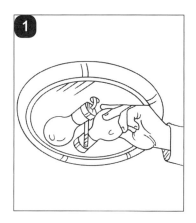

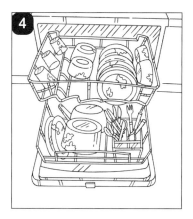

1. _____*lightbulb*_____   3. _____

2. _____   4. _____

B Number the sentences in the correct order.

_1_ Mrs. Chan's washing machine was leaking.

____ The neighbor called the building manager.

____ Mrs. Chan thanked her neighbor the next day.

____ Mrs. Chan was very happy.

____ Mrs. Chan's neighbor saw water under the door.

____ The building manager called a plumber.

____ The plumber came and fixed the leak.

Lesson B *Which one do you recommend?*

A Read the cards. Circle the correct answers.

HELPING HANDS
Plumbing, electric, and much more!

Work is guaranteed.
Cash Only. No credit cards.
12 years of experience
Insured
$60 an hour
Tel: 555-5599

Handy Repair Service
Plumbing and electrical repairs

24 hours a day
We take all major credit cards.
24 years of experience
Licensed
$75 an hour
Tel: 555-4497

1. Which service is insured?   (Helping Hands)   Handy Repair Service

2. Which service is more experienced?   Helping Hands   Handy Repair Service

3. Which service is cheaper?   Helping Hands   Handy Repair Service

4. Which service takes credit cards?   Helping Hands   Handy Repair Service

5. Which service is open 24 hours a day?   Helping Hands   Handy Repair Service

B Write questions.

1. My sink is leaking.

   Which / you / do / recommend / plumber

   Which plumber do you recommend _____ ?

2. We need to buy some food.

   Which / you / do / like / supermarket

   _____ ?

3. I want to find a new bank.

   Which / recommend / you / do / bank

   _____ ?

4. I need new shoes.

   Which / do / you / suggest / department store

   _____ ?

C Complete the sentences. Recommend stores or services in your own community.

   1. (coffee shop) I recommend _____

   2. (drugstore) I recommend _____

Name: _____

Lesson B *Which one do you recommend?*

A Read the cards. Circle *T* (true) or *F* (false). Correct the false sentences.

HELPING HANDS
Plumbing, electric, and much more!

Work is guaranteed.
Cash Only. No credit cards.
12 years of experience
Insured
$60 an hour
Tel: 555-5599

Handy Repair Service
Plumbing and electrical repairs

24 hours a day
We take all major credit cards.
24 years of experience
Licensed
$75 an hour
Tel: 555-4497

1. Helping Hands is not insured.   T (F) *Helping Hands is insured.*

2. Helping Hands is more experienced.   T   F   _____

3. Handy Repair Service is cheaper.   T   F   _____

4. Handy Repair Service takes credit cards. T   F   _____

5. Helping Hands is open 24 hours a day.   T   F   _____

B Complete the questions.

1. My sink is leaking. Which plumber *do you recommend* _____ ?
   (recommend)

2. We need to buy some food. Which supermarket _____ ?
   (like)

3. I want to find a new bank. Which bank _____ ?
   (recommend)

4. I need new shoes. Which department store _____ ?
   (suggest)

C Complete the conversations. Recommend stores or services in your own community to a friend.

1. **Your friend** I need to find a good coffee shop.

   You _____

2. **Your friend** I need to find a drugstore.

   You _____

Name: _____

Lesson B *Which one do you recommend?*

A Read the cards. Answer the questions.

HELPING HANDS
Plumbing, electric, and much more!

Work is guaranteed.
Cash Only. No credit cards.
12 years of experience
Insured
$60 an hour
Tel: 555-5599

Handy Repair Service
Plumbing and electrical repairs

24 hours a day
We take all major credit cards.
24 years of experience
Licensed
$75 an hour
Tel: 555-4497

1. Which service is insured? *Helping Hands is insured.* _____

2. Which service is more experienced? _____

3. Which service is cheaper? _____

4. Which service takes credit cards? _____

5. Which service is open 24 hours a day? _____

B Write questions. Use *Which* and the simple present.

1. My sink is leaking. *Which plumber do you recommend?* _____
   (plumber / recommend)

2. We need to buy some food. _____
   (supermarket / like)

3. I want to find a new bank. _____
   (bank / recommend)

4. I need new shoes. _____
   (department store / suggest)

C Complete the conversations. Recommend stores or services in your own
community to a friend. Give reasons.

1. **Your friend** I need to find a good coffee shop.

   You _____

   _____

2. **Your friend** I need to find a drugstore.

   You _____

   _____

Lesson C *Can you call a plumber, please?*

A What are the problems in this bathroom? Make a list.

floor	lightbulb	sink	toilet	window

1. fix the *window* _____
2. change the _____
3. clean the _____
4. fix the _____
5. unclog the _____

B Match the sentences with the requests.

1. The dishes are dirty.
2. The stove is broken.
3. The lock is broken.
4. I need to dry my clothes.
5. The light isn't working.
6. The sink is clogged.

a. Could you fix the lock, please?
b. Would you repair the dishwasher, please?
c. Can you unclog the sink, please?
d. Could you call an electrician, please?
e. Can you repair the stove, please?
f. Will you fix the dryer, please?

C Complete the word maps.

I can't right now.	I'd be happy to.	Maybe later.	Of course.	Sorry.	Sure.

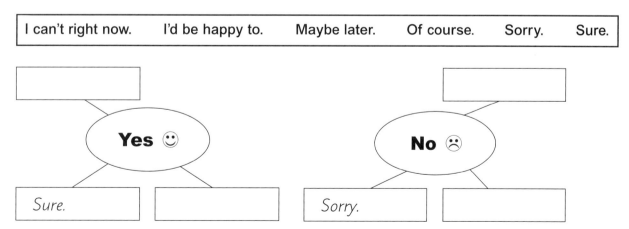

Lesson C *Can you call a plumber, please?*

A What are the problems in this bathroom? Make a list. Use some words more than once.

change	clean	fix	unclog

1. *fix the window* _____
2. _____
3. _____
4. _____
5. _____

B Complete the questions.

call an electrician	fix the lock	repair the stove
fix the dryer	repair the dishwasher	unclog the sink

1. The dishes are dirty. Would you *repair the dishwasher* _____ , please?

2. The stove is broken. Can you _____ , please?

3. The lock is broken. Could you _____ , please?

4. I need to dry my clothes. Will you _____ , please?

5. The light isn't working. Could you _____ , please?

6. The sink is clogged. Can you _____ , please?

C Complete the word maps.

I can't right now.	I'm busy.	No problem.	Sorry.
I'd be happy to.	Maybe later.	Of course.	Sure.

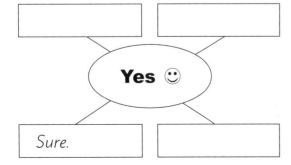

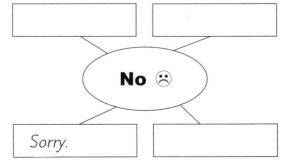

Name: _____

Lesson C *Can you call a plumber, please?*

A What are the problems in this bathroom? Make a list.

1. *fix the window* _____
2. _____
3. _____
4. _____
5. _____

B Complete the questions.

1. The dishes are dirty. Would you repair *the dishwasher* _____ , please?

2. The stove is broken. Can you repair _____ , please?

3. The lock is broken. Could you fix _____ , please?

4. I need to dry my clothes. Will you fix _____ , please?

5. The light isn't working. Could you call _____ , please?

6. The sink is clogged. Can you unclog _____ , please?

C Complete the word maps. Add your own ideas.

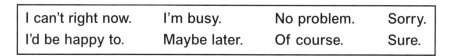

| I can't right now. | I'm busy. | No problem. | Sorry. |
| I'd be happy to. | Maybe later. | Of course. | Sure. |

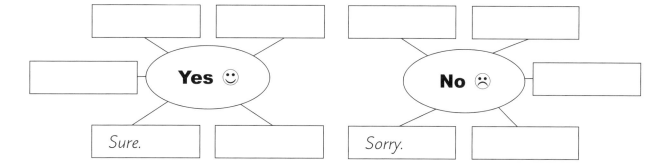

Yes ☺

Sure.

No ☹

Sorry.

Lesson D Reading

A Look at the pictures. Circle the answers.

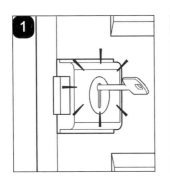

The lock is ___ .

a. torn

b. jammed

The chair is ___ .

a. stained

b. cracked

The window is ___ .

a. bent

b. cracked

The table is ___ .

a. stained

b. bent

B Read the problems. Match the sentence parts.

Sunny View Apartments		
Floor	**Location**	**Problem**
1st floor	Laundry room	The washing machine is leaking.
2nd floor	Hall	The hall has a burned-out light.
2nd floor	Apartment 203	The sink is clogged.
3rd floor	Apartment 305	The bathroom window is broken.

1. The tenant in Apartment 305

2. There is a leaking washing machine

3. The hall on the second floor

4. The sink is clogged

a. has a burned-out light.

b. has a broken window.

c. in Apartment 203.

d. in the laundry room.

C Complete the request for each problem.

call a plumber   call a repair person   change the lightbulb   fix the window

1. The washing machine is leaking. Could you _call a repair person_ , please?

2. The hall has a burned-out light. Could you _____ , please?

3. The sink is clogged. Could you _____ , please?

4. The bathroom window is broken. Could you _____ , please?

Lesson D *Reading*

A Look at the pictures. Complete the sentences.

bent	cracked	jammed	stained

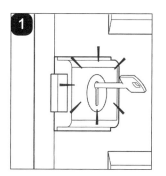 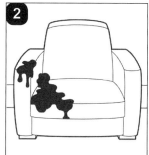  

The lock is   The chair is   The window is   The table is

____*jammed*____ .   _____ .   _____ .   _____ .

B Read the problems. Complete the sentences.

Sunny View Apartments		
Floor	**Location**	**Problem**
1st floor	Laundry room	The washing machine is leaking.
2nd floor	Hall	The hall has a burned-out light.
2nd floor	Apartment 203	The sink is clogged.
3rd floor	Apartment 305	The bathroom window is broken.

1. The tenant in Apartment 305 *has a broken window* _____ .

2. There is a leaking washing machine _____ .

3. The hall on the second floor _____ .

4. The sink is clogged _____ .

C Make a request for each problem. Use *Could*.

call a plumber	call a repair person	change the lightbulb	fix the window

1. The washing machine is leaking. *Could you call a repair person, please?*

2. The hall has a burned-out light. _____

3. The sink is clogged. _____

4. The bathroom window is broken. _____

Lesson D Reading

A Look at the pictures. Complete the sentences.

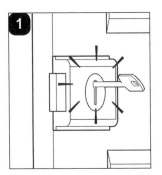  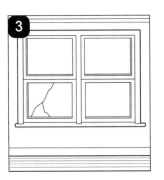 

| 1 | 2 | 3 | 4 |

The lock is   The chair is   The window is   The table is

_____jammed_____ .   _____ .   _____ .   _____ .

B Read the problems. Answer the questions.

Sunny View Apartments		
Floor	**Location**	**Problem**
1st floor	Laundry room	The washing machine is leaking.
2nd floor	Hall	The hall has a burned-out light.
2nd floor	Apartment 203	The sink is clogged.
3rd floor	Apartment 305	The bathroom window is broken.
4th floor	Apartment 408	The back door is jammed.

1. Which tenant has a broken window? _the tenant in Apartment 305_

2. Where is the leaking washing machine? _____

3. What's the problem in the hall? _____

4. What's the problem in Apartment 203? _____

5. Which tenant has a jammed door? _____

C Make a request for each problem. Use *Could*.

1. The washing machine is leaking. _Could you call a repair person, please?_

2. The hall has a burned-out light. _____

3. The sink is clogged. _____

4. The bathroom window is broken. _____

5. The back door is jammed. _____

Lesson **E** *Writing*

A Complete the letter.

1. _____date_____ **April 10, 2008**

2. _____ Dear Building _____ ,

                                           (Manager / Neighbor)

       I am a _____ at _____ .

               (tenant / landlord)   (469 W. Main St. / an apartment building)

   I am writing to you about _____ in my

                           (people / problems)

   apartment. I am very _____ . The ceiling is

                    (happy / upset)

3. _____ _____ water. The washing machine and dryer are

      (leaking / jammed)

   broken. The window is also _____ . Could you please

                        (cracked / burned out)

   send a _____ right away? You can contact me in

       (tenant / repair person)

   Apartment 2C if you have any questions. Thank you for your attention.

4. _____ Sincerely,

5. _____ *Armen Krikorian*

   Armen Krikorian

B Circle the answers. Use the information from Exercise A.

1. What is the date of this letter?

   (a. April 10, 2008)   b. 469 W. Main St.

2. Who is the letter to?

   a. the building manager   b. a neighbor

3. Who is the letter from?

   a. the building manager   b. a tenant

4. What is the letter about?

   a. problems in the apartment   b. problems with neighbors

C Label the parts of the letter in Exercise A.

body	closing	date	opening	signature

Lesson **E** *Writing*

A Complete the letter.

469 W. Main St.	cracked	Manager	repair person	upset
April 10, 2008	leaking	problems	tenant	

1. ___date___ ⎰ April 10, 2008 _____

2. _____ ⎰ Dear Building _____ ,

3. _____ ⎰   I am a _____ at _____ . I am
writing to you about _____ in my apartment. I am
very _____ . The ceiling is _____
water. The washing machine and dryer are broken. The window
is also _____ . Could you please send a
_____ right away? You can contact me in Apartment
2C if you have any questions. Thank you for your attention.

4. _____ ⎰ Sincerely,

5. _____ ⎰ *Armen Krikorian*
Armen Krikorian

B Complete the sentences. Use the information from Exercise A.

1. The date of this letter is *April 10, 2008* _____ .

2. The letter is to _____ .

3. The letter is from _____ .

4. The letter is about _____ .

C Label the parts of the letter in Exercise A.

body	closing	date	opening	signature

Lesson E *Writing*

A Write the information in the correct order to make a letter.

- April 10, 2008
- Could you please send a repair person right away?
- I am a tenant at 469 W. Main St.
- You can contact me in Apartment 2C if you have any questions. Thank you for your attention.
- Dear Building Manager,
- The ceiling is leaking water. The washing machine and dryer are broken.
- The window is also cracked.
- I am writing to you about problems in my apartment. I am very upset.

1. ___date___   *April 10, 2008* _____

2. _____ _____

3. _____
_____
_____
_____
_____
_____
_____
_____
_____
_____

4. _____ Sincerely,

5. _____ *Armen Krikorian*
Armen Krikorian

B Answer the questions. Use the information from Exercise A.

1. What is the date of this letter? *April 10, 2008* _____

2. Who is the letter to? _____

3. Who is the letter from? _____

4. What is the letter about? _____

C Label the parts of the letter in Exercise A.

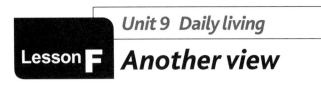

A Look at the invoice. Circle the answers.

Miller's General Home Repairs
Green Bay, Wisconsin 54311
(920) 555–1234

Customer Name: _Mrs. Delgado_
Customer Address: _3147 Bedford Road_   **Apartment**: _6D_
Tel: _920-555-3102_
Service Technician: _Steve_

Description of problem	Repairs made	Actual cost
Broken dryer	Fixed dryer	$80
Cracked window	New window	$48
Broken door	New door	$100
Clogged sink	Unclogged sink	$60
	TOTAL	

1. How much did it cost to fix the dryer?

   (a. $80)   b. $48   c. $120

2. What was cracked?

   a. the door   b. the window   c. the sink

3. Which repair was the most expensive?

   a. the sink   b. the door   c. the dryer

4. Which repair was the cheapest?

   a. the sink   b. the dryer   c. the window

5. How much is the total?

   a. $208   b. $236   c. $288

B Match the home problems with the correct repair person.

1. You have a broken lock.   a. a carpenter

2. Your sink is leaking.   b. an electrician

3. Your door is broken.   c. a locksmith

4. You have a stain on your wall.   d. a painter

5. There is a problem with your lights. e. a plumber

Lesson F Another view

A Look at the invoice. Answer the questions.

Miller's General Home Repairs
Green Bay, Wisconsin 54311
(920) 555–1234

Customer Name: _Mrs. Delgado_

Customer Address: _3147 Bedford Road_   **Apartment:** _6D_

Tel: _920-555-3102_

Service Technician: _Steve_

Description of problem	Repairs made	Actual cost
Broken dryer	Fixed dryer	$80
Cracked window	New window	$48
Broken door	New door	$100
Clogged sink	Unclogged sink	$60
	TOTAL	

1. How much did it cost to fix the dryer? _$80_____

2. What was cracked? _____

3. Which repair was the most expensive? _____

4. Which repair was the cheapest? _____

5. How much is the total? _____

B Complete the sentences.

a carpenter   an electrician   a locksmith   a painter   a plumber

1. You have a broken lock. You need _a locksmith_____ .

2. Your sink is leaking. You need _____ .

3. Your door is broken. You need _____ .

4. You have a stain on your wall. You need _____ .

5. There is a problem with your lights. You need _____ .

Lesson F *Another view*

A Look at the invoice. Complete the questions and write the answers.

Miller's General Home Repairs
Green Bay, Wisconsin 54311
(920) 555–1234

Customer Name: *Mrs. Delgado*
Customer Address: *3147 Bedford Road*   **Apartment**: *6D*
Tel: *920-555-3102*
Service Technician: *Steve*

Description of problem	Repairs made	Actual cost
Broken dryer	Fixed dryer	$80
Cracked window	New window	$48
Broken door	New door	$100
Clogged sink	Unclogged sink	$60
	TOTAL	

1. How much _____*did it cost to fix*_____ the dryer? _____*$80*_____

2. What _____ cracked? _____

3. Which repair _____ the most expensive? _____

4. Which repair _____ the cheapest? _____

5. How much _____ the total? _____

B Complete the sentences. Write the correct repair person.

1. You have a broken lock. You need *a locksmith* .

2. Your sink is leaking. You need _____ .

3. Your door is broken. You need _____ .

4. You have a stain on your wall. You need _____ .

5. There is a problem with your lights. You need _____ .

Lesson A *Get ready*

A Look at the clues. Complete the puzzle.

balloons	cake	card	flowers	party	perfume	present

Across

1  **3**  **5** 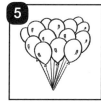 **6**

Down

1  **2**

4

B Complete the sentences. Use words from Exercise A.

1. I had a _p_ _a_ _r_ _t_ _y_ with my friends and family.

2. We put _b_ ___ ___ ___ ___ ___ ___ ___ around the room.
   They looked great!

3. My sister made a chocolate _c_ ___ ___ ___ .

4. Everyone gave me a birthday _c_ ___ ___ ___ .

5. My friend gave me a bottle of _p_ ___ ___ ___ ___ ___ ___ .
   It smells nice.

6. My parents gave me very pretty _f_ ___ ___ ___ ___ ___ ___ .
   They smell good.

C Write one sentence about your last birthday. What happened?

_____

Lesson A *Get ready*

A Look at the clues. Complete the puzzle.

Across

Down

```
            ¹p e r ²f u m e
                    
        ³_ _ _       _
                    _
                    _
            ⁴_
        ⁵_ _ _ _ _ _
            _
    ⁶_ _ _ _ _ _
```

B Complete the sentences. Use words from Exercise A.

1. I had a p _arty_____ with my friends and family.

2. We put b_____ around the room. They looked great!

3. My sister made a chocolate c_____ .

4. Everyone gave me a birthday c_____ .

5. My friend gave me a bottle of p_____ . It smells nice.

6. My parents gave me very pretty f_____ . They smell good.

C Write two sentences about your last birthday. What happened?

_____

_____

Lesson A *Get ready*

Name: _____

A Look at the clues. Complete the puzzle.

Across

Down

B Complete the sentences. Use words from Exercise A.

1. I had a _____*party*_____ with my friends and family.

2. We put _____ around the room. They looked great!

3. My sister made a chocolate _____ .

4. Everyone gave me a birthday _____ .

5. My friend gave me a bottle of _____ . It smells nice.

6. My parents gave me very pretty _____ . They smell good.

C Write three sentences about your last birthday. What happened?

_____

_____

_____

Name: _____

Lesson B *Would you like some cake?*

A Complete the conversations.

1. **A** Would they like some cake?

   B Yes, *they would* .

2. **A** Would she like a cup of tea?

   B Yes, _____ .

3. **A** Would he like a bottle of water?

   B Yes, _____ .

4. **A** Would you like some dessert?

   B No, _____ .

5. **A** Would you like some soda?

   B No, _____ .

B Complete the conversations.

cheese	cookies	fruit	pie

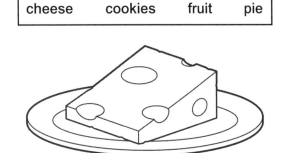

1. **A** What would you like?

   B I'd like some *cheese* .

2. **A** What would he like?

   B He'd like some _____ .

3. **A** What would she like?

   B She'd like a piece of _____ .

4. **A** What would they like?

   B They'd like some _____ .

Name: _____

Lesson **B** *Would you like some cake?*

A Complete the conversations.

1. **A** <u>*Would they like*</u> some cake?
          (they)

   B Yes, <u>*they would*</u> .

2. **A** _____ a cup of tea?
          (she)

   B Yes, _____ .

3. **A** _____ a bottle of water?
          (he)

   B Yes, _____ .

4. **A** _____ some dessert?
          (you)

   B No, _____ .

5. **A** _____ some soda?
          (you)

   B No, _____ .

B Look at the pictures. Complete the conversations.

cheese	cookies	fruit	pie

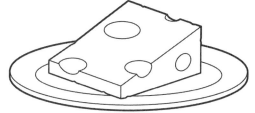

1. **A** What would you like?

   B <u>*I'd like*</u> some <u>*cheese*</u> .

2. **A** What would he like?

   B _____ some _____ .

3. **A** What would she like?

   B _____ a piece of _____ .

4. **A** What would they like?

   B _____ some _____ .

Name: _____

Lesson B *Would you like some cake?*

A Complete the conversations.

1. **A** _Would they like_ some cake?
   (they)
   B Yes, _they would_ .

2. **A** _____ a cup of tea?
   (she)
   B Yes, _____ .

3. **A** _____ a bottle of water?
   (he)
   B Yes, _____ .

4. **A** _____ some dessert?
   (you)
   B No, _____ .

5. **A** _____ some soda?
   (you)
   B No, _____ .

B Look at the pictures. Complete the conversations.

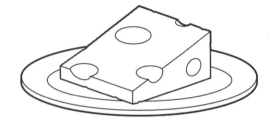

1. **A** What would you like?
   B _I'd like_ some _cheese_ .

2. **A** What would he like?
   B _____ some _____ .

3. **A** What would she like?
   B _____ a piece of _____ .

4. **A** What would they like?
   B _____ some _____ .

Lesson C *Tim gave Mary a present.*

A Complete the sentences.

1. **A** What did Tito buy Mary?

   B Tito bought _____*Mary*_____ some flowers.

2. **A** What did Allie and Claire send Harry?

   B Allie and Claire sent _____ a letter.

3. **A** What did Lucia give John?

   B Lucia gave _____ some books.

4. **A** What did Kong bring for Yoshi and Naomi?

   B Kong brought _____ some cookies.

B Circle the correct sentences.

1. What did Tito buy Mary?

   a. Tito bought her some flowers.   b. Tito bought them some flowers.

2. What did Allie and Claire send Harry?

   a. Allie and Claire sent her a letter.   b. Allie and Claire sent him a letter.

3. What did Lucia give John?

   a. Lucia gave him some books.   b. Lucia gave her some books.

4. What did Kong bring for Yoshi and Naomi?

   a. Kong brought him some cookies.   b. Kong brought them some cookies.

C Circle the correct pronoun.

1. Susana likes Claudia and Lorenzo.

   Susana likes ___ .

   a. they   b. them

2. Claudia and Lorenzo like Susana.

   Claudia and Lorenzo like ___ .

   a. she   b. her

3. Claudia likes Lorenzo.

   Claudia likes ___ .

   a. him   b. he

4. Lorenzo likes Susana and Claudia.

   Lorenzo likes ___ .

   a. she   b. them

Lesson C *Tim gave Mary a present.*

A Rewrite the sentences.

1. Tito bought some flowers for Mary.

   Tito bought *Mary some flowers* _____ .

2. Allie and Claire sent a letter to Harry.

   Allie and Claire sent _____ .

3. Lucia gave some books to John.

   Lucia gave _____ .

4. Kong brought some cookies for Yoshi and Naomi.

   Kong brought _____ .

B Complete the answers. Use the information from Exercise A. Use *him*, *her*, or *them*.

1. What did Tito buy Mary?

   Tito bought ___*her*___ some flowers.

2. What did Allie and Claire send Harry?

   Allie and Claire sent _____ a letter.

3. What did Lucia give John?

   Lucia gave _____ some books.

4. What did Kong bring for Yoshi and Naomi?

   Kong brought _____ some cookies.

C Complete the sentences. Use *him*, *her*, or *them*.

1. Susana likes Claudia and Lorenzo.

   Susana likes ___*them*___ .

2. Claudia and Lorenzo like Susana.

   Claudia and Lorenzo like _____ .

3. Claudia likes Lorenzo.

   Claudia likes _____ .

4. Lorenzo likes Susana and Claudia.

   Lorenzo likes _____ .

Lesson C *Tim gave Mary a present.*

A Rewrite the sentences.

1. Tito bought some flowers for Mary.

   Tito bought Mary some flowers. _____

2. Allie and Claire sent a letter to Harry.

   _____

3. Lucia gave some books to John.

   _____

4. Kong brought some cookies for Yoshi and Naomi.

   _____

B Answer the questions. Use the information from Exercise A. Use *him*, *her*, or *them*.

1. What did Tito buy Mary?

   Tito bought her some flowers. _____

2. What did Allie and Claire send Harry?

   _____

3. What did Lucia give John?

   _____

4. What did Kong bring for Yoshi and Naomi?

   _____

C Rewrite the sentences. Use *him*, *her*, or *them*.

1. Susana likes Claudia and Lorenzo.

   Susana likes them. _____

2. Claudia and Lorenzo like Susana.

   _____

3. Claudia likes Lorenzo.

   _____

4. Lorenzo likes Susana and Claudia.

   _____

Name: _____

Lesson D *Reading*

A Complete the sentences.

1. You eat turkey on _____*Thanksgiving*_____ .
   (Thanksgiving / Valentine's Day)

2. You give flowers to your mother on _____ .
   (Mother's Day / Halloween)

3. You give chocolates to your wife or husband on _____ .
   (Independence Day / Valentine's Day)

4. You bring gifts for a baby to a _____ .
   (baby shower / housewarming)

5. You celebrate the end of the year on _____ .
   (New Year's Eve / Halloween)

6. You bring gifts for the home to a _____ .
   (baby shower / housewarming)

B Read the paragraph. Match the questions with the answers.

Denise had a birthday party last Saturday. She sent invitations to her classmates and her relatives. They all came to the party. Her classmates gave her a big birthday card. Her sister gave her a book. Her mother brought food and drinks to the party. Her grandparents brought flowers and perfume. After the party, Denise wrote thank-you notes to everyone.

1. When was Denise's birthday party?   a. a book

2. Who came to the party?   b. her mother

3. Who gave her flowers and perfume?   c. last Saturday

4. Who brought food and drinks?   d. her grandparents

5. What did Denise's sister give her?   e. She wrote thank-you notes.

6. What did Denise do after the party?   f. her classmates and relatives

Lesson D *Reading*

A Complete the sentences.

baby shower	Mother's Day	Thanksgiving
housewarming	New Year's Eve	Valentine's Day

1. You eat turkey on *Thanksgiving*   .

2. You give flowers to your mother on _____ .

3. You give chocolates to your wife or husband on _____ .

4. You bring gifts for a baby to a _____ .

5. You celebrate the end of the year on _____ .

6. You bring gifts for the home to a _____ .

B Read the paragraph. Answer the questions.

    Denise had a birthday party last Saturday. She sent invitations to her classmates and her relatives. They all came to the party. Her classmates gave her a big birthday card. Her sister gave her a book. Her mother brought food and drinks to the party. Her grandparents brought flowers and perfume. After the party, Denise wrote thank-you notes to everyone.

1. When was Denise's birthday party? *last Saturday* _____

2. Who came to the party? _____

3. Who gave her flowers and perfume? _____

4. Who brought food and drinks? _____

5. What did Denise's sister give her? _____

6. What did Denise do after the party? _____

Lesson D *Reading*

A Complete the sentences with the names of celebrations.

1. You eat turkey on *Thanksgiving* _____ .

2. You give flowers to your mother on _____ .

3. You give chocolates to your wife or husband on _____ .

4. You bring gifts for a baby to a _____ .

5. You celebrate the end of the year on _____ .

6. You bring gifts for the home to a _____ .

B Read the paragraph and the answers. Write questions.

Denise had a birthday party last Saturday. She sent invitations to her classmates and her relatives. They all came to the party. Her classmates gave her a big birthday card. Her sister gave her a book. Her mother brought food and drinks to the party. Her grandparents brought flowers and perfume. After the party, Denise wrote thank-you notes to everyone.

1. When *was Denise's birthday party* _____ ? last Saturday

2. Who came _____ ? her classmates and relatives

3. Who gave _____ ? her grandparents

4. Who brought _____ ? her mother

5. What _____ ? a book

6. What _____ ? She wrote thank-you notes.

A Read the thank-you notes. Answer the questions.

March 23, 2008 *Dear Mrs. Kramer,* *I want to thank you for the backpack you gave me for my birthday. I really like the color. Orange is my favorite color.* *Thank you so much for coming to my birthday party. I hope you had a good time.* *Sincerely,* *Mario Lozano*	*March 23, 2008* *Dear Uncle Tony and Aunt Donna,* *Thank you for the new dictionary you gave me for my birthday. It will help me a lot in English class next year.* *Thank you so much for coming to my birthday party. I hope you had a good time.* *Love,* *Mario*

1. What did Mrs. Kramer give Mario? _____ *a backpack* _____
(a backpack / a dictionary)

2. What did his relatives give him? _____
(a backpack / a dictionary)

3. Why did Mario like the backpack? _____
(He liked the color. / It will help him in English class.)

4. Why did Mario like the dictionary? _____
(He liked the color. / It will help him in English class.)

5. When did he write the thank-you notes? _____
(on March 23, 2007 / on March 23, 2008)

B You had a graduation party last week. Your friend gave you a new watch.
Write a thank-you note.

_____ , _____

Dear _____ ,

Thank you for the _____ *you gave me for*
_____ . *I really like it, and I wear it every day.*

Thank you so much for coming to my _____ . *I*
hope you had a good time.

_____ ,

_____

Lesson E Writing

■ ✓ ■

A Read the thank-you notes. Answer the questions.

March 23, 2008

Dear Mrs. Kramer,

    I want to thank you for the backpack you gave me for my birthday. I really like the color. Orange is my favorite color.
    Thank you so much for coming to my birthday party. I hope you had a good time.

Sincerely,

Mario Lozano

March 23, 2008

Dear Uncle Tony and Aunt Donna,

    Thank you for the new dictionary you gave me for my birthday. It will help me a lot in English class next year.
    Thank you so much for coming to my birthday party. I hope you had a good time.

Love,

Mario

1. What did Mrs. Kramer give Mario? *a backpack* _____

2. What did his relatives give him? _____

3. Why did Mario like the backpack? _____

4. Why did Mario like the dictionary? _____

5. When did he write the thank-you notes? _____

B You had a graduation party last week. Your friend gave you a new watch.
Write a thank-you note.

_____ , _____

Dear _____ ,

    Thank you _____ you gave me for

_____ . I really like it, and I wear it every day.

    Thank you so much for _____ . I hope you

had _____ .

_____ ,

_____

A Read the thank-you notes. Read the answers. Complete the questions.

March 23, 2008

Dear Mrs. Kramer,

   I want to thank you for the backpack you gave me for my birthday. I really like the color. Orange is my favorite color.

   Thank you so much for coming to my birthday party. I hope you had a good time.

Sincerely,

Mario Lozano

March 23, 2008

Dear Uncle Tony and Aunt Donna,

   Thank you for the new dictionary you gave me for my birthday. It will help me a lot in English class next year.

   Thank you so much for coming to my birthday party. I hope you had a good time.

Love,

Mario

---

1. What *did Mrs. Kramer give Mario* _____ ?   a backpack

2. What _____ ?   a dictionary

3. Why _____ ?   He liked the color.

4. Why _____ ?   It will help him in English class.

5. When _____ ?   on March 23, 2008

B You had a graduation party last week. Your friend gave you a new watch.
Write a thank-you note.

   _____ , _____

Dear _____ ,

   Thank you _____ .

I really like it, and I wear it every day.

   Thank you so much for _____ .

I hope _____ .

   _____ ,

   _____

Name: _____

Lesson F Another view

A Look at the invitation. Circle the answers.

> ## SHHH!
> ### IT'S A SECRET!
> A Surprise Baby Shower
> for Ana Maria Garcia
>
> **Given by:** Michelle Wassem and Lois Smith
> **Date:** Sunday, June 3
> **Time:** 2:00 p.m. until 5:00 p.m.
> **Place:** 345 Third St., Apt. 3B
> **RSVP** (212) 555-8890 by May 21

1. Who is the shower for?

   a. Ana Maria Garcia

   b. Lois Smith

   c. Michelle Wassem

2. Who is giving the party?

   a. Ana Maria Garcia and Michelle Wassem

   b. Lois Smith and Ana Maria Garcia

   c. Michelle Wassem and Lois Smith

3. When do people need to say *yes* or *no* to the invitation?

   a. by May 21

   b. on June 3

   c. at 2:00 p.m.

4. When is the party?

   a. on May 21

   b. on June 3

   c. in Apt. 3B

B You are going to have a party next month. Write an invitation.

IT'S A PARTY!
Please join us!

For: _____
(Write the special occasion.)

Date: _____
(Write the day of the party.)

Time: _____ until _____
(When the party begins) (When the party ends)

Place: _____
(Where will you have the party?)

RSVP: _____
(When do people need to say yes or no?)

Lesson F *Another view*

A Look at the invitation. Rewrite the false sentences.

> ### SHHH!
> #### IT'S A SECRET!
> ## A Surprise Baby Shower for Ana Maria Garcia
>
> **Given by:** *Michelle Wassem and Lois Smith*
> **Date:** *Sunday, June 3*
> **Time:** *2:00 p.m. until 5:00 p.m.*
> **Place:** *345 Third St., Apt. 3B*
> **RSVP** *(212) 555-8890 by May 21*

1. The shower is for ~~Michelle Wassem and Lois Smith~~.

    The shower is for Ana Maria Garcia.

2. Ana Maria Garcia is giving the party.

    _____

3. People need to say *yes* or *no* to the invitation by June 3.

    _____

4. The party is on May 21.

    _____

B You are going to have a party next month. Write an invitation.

> ## IT'S A PARTY!
> ### Please join us!
>
> **For:** _____
>
> **Date:** _____
>
> **Time:** _____ **until** _____
>
> **Place:** _____
>
> **RSVP:** _____

Lesson F | *Another view*

A Look at the invitation. Answer the questions.

> ### SHHH!
> IT'S A SECRET!
> A Surprise Baby Shower
> for Ana Maria Garcia
>
> **Given by:** *Michelle Wassem and Lois Smith*
> **Date:** *Sunday, June 3*
> **Time:** *2:00 p.m. until 5:00 p.m.*
> **Place:** *345 Third St., Apt. 3B*
> **RSVP** *(212) 555-8890 by May 21*

1. Who is the shower for? *The shower is for Ana Maria Garcia.*

2. Who is giving the party? _____

3. When do people need to say *yes* or *no* to the invitation? _____

4. When is the party? _____

B You are going to have a party next month. Write an invitation.

> ### IT'S A PARTY!
> Please join us!
>
> For: _____
>
> Date: _____
>
> Time: _____ until _____
>
> Place: _____
>
> RSVP: _____

Answer key

Unit 1: Personal information

Lesson A: Get ready pages 1–3

A

1. Lisa has long curly hair. She is wearing a striped shirt.
2. Bill has short straight hair. He is wearing black shoes.
3. Sue has short curly hair. She is wearing a black skirt.
4. Eva has long straight hair. She is wearing a black shirt.
5. José has short curly hair. He is wearing a soccer uniform.

B

1. Ann has short curly hair. She is wearing a black shirt.
2. Tom has long straight hair. He is wearing a striped shirt.
3. Jim has short straight hair. He is wearing a soccer uniform.

C

Answers will vary.

Lesson B: She's wearing a short plaid skirt. pages 4–6

A

1. large checked pants
2. large checked shirt
3. short plaid coat
4. long striped socks

B

1. a large red backpack
2. a small purple coat
3. a black plaid skirt
4. green striped socks

C

1. a large checked shirt
2. a short black dress
3. a small blue sweater
4. long striped pants
5. a small plaid suit
6. short brown boots

Lesson C: What are you doing right now? pages 7–9

A

1. Eduardo is playing soccer.
2. Ivana studies English.
3. Lin is studying English.

4. Eduardo plays soccer.
5. They are watching TV.

B

1A. What does Lin do on Sunday?
1B. She rests.
2A. What does Eduardo do on Thursday?
2B. He goes to class.
3A. What do Eduardo and Lin do on Tuesday?
3B. They do homework.
4A. What is Ivana doing right now?
4B. She is cleaning the house.

C

Answers will vary.

Lesson D: Reading pages 10–12

A

1. bracelet, earrings, purse
2. watch, gloves, necklace
3. scarf, hat, earrings
4. ring, scarf, tie

B

1. She's 20 years old.
2. She studies computers.
3. She plays soccer every week.
4. She goes hiking on the weekend.
5. She usually wears jeans.
6. She is wearing a dress.

Lesson E: Writing pages 13–15

A

1. Dan has short straight hair.
2. Dan is wearing a striped shirt.
3. Dave has short curly hair.
4. Dave is wearing a plaid shirt.

B

1. on the weekend
2. on Thursday night
3. after class
4. on the weekend
5. after class

C

Dan and Dave are brothers. Dan has short straight hair. Dave has short curly hair. On Thursday night, Dan watches

movies. He fixes things in the house on the weekend. Dave goes to the supermarket after class. On Thursday night, he plays basketball.

Lesson F: Another view pages 16–18

A

1. $39
2. $15
3. $57
4. $50

B

156B: 1, large, green, sweater, $39
288C: 3 pairs, medium, blue, socks, $15
478A: 1, extra large, green, coat, $57
560F: 2 pairs, 7, red, shoes, $50
Total: $161

C

111B: 1, small, purple, sweater, $48
452C: 5 pairs, large, black, socks, $35
344A: 2 pairs, 9, brown, shoes, $106
650F: 1, medium, blue, jacket, $29
Total: $218

Unit 2: At school

Lesson A: Get ready pages 19–21

A

1. a computer lab
2. a mouse
3. a monitor
4. a keyboard
5. a lab instructor
6. a hall

B

1. Miho is taking a keyboarding class.
2. Miho wrote the e-mail in the computer lab.
3. Miho thinks the class is going to help her in college.
4. Larry Smith is Miho's lab instructor.

Lesson B: What do you want to do? pages 22–24

A

1. What do you want to do? I want to get a job.
2. What does he want to do? He wants to become a citizen.
3. What do they need to do? They need to study auto mechanics.
4. What does she need to do? She needs to go to college.

B

1. He needs to take driving lessons.
2. I need to take a citizenship class.
3. They need to take a computer class.
4. He needs to get a second job.
5. She needs to take a GED class.

C

1. You could take a cooking class.
2. Why don't you take driving lessons?
3. You could take a citizenship class.
4. Why don't you talk to a counselor?
5. Why don't you study auto mechanics?

D

Answers will vary.

Lesson C: What will you do? pages 25–27

A

1. Maybe she will buy a house.
2. He will most likely learn a new language.
3. She will probably go to college.
4. He will probably open a business.

B

1. Pat won't do homework on Tuesday morning.
2. She will work on Tuesday morning.
3. She will go to English class on Monday afternoon.
4. She won't work on Wednesday morning.
5. She won't go to English class on Monday morning.

Lesson D: Reading pages 28–30

A

1. culinary arts
2. landscape design
3. nursing
4. accounting

B

1. Bettina's goal is to open a hotel.
2. Bettina has to take three steps.
3. The second step is to study hotel management.
4. The third step is to work in a hotel.
5. She wants to reach her goal in five or six years.

C

Answers will vary.

Lesson E: Writing pages 31–33

A

His goal is to own a restaurant. He needs to: 1) study culinary arts; 2) work as a cook in three or four different restaurants; 3) take business classes. He wants to reach his goal in ten years.

B

1. My name is Karen.
2. My goal is to go to nursing school.
3. There are three steps I need to take to reach my goal.
4. First, I need to speak, read, and write English better.
5. Second, I need to talk to nurses to learn more about what they do.
6. Third, I need to talk to a counselor about nursing schools.
7. Maybe I'll be ready to start nursing school next year.

C

1. Karen's goal is to go to nursing school.
2. First, she needs to speak, read, and write English better.
3. Second, she needs to talk to nurses.
4. Third, she needs to talk to a counselor about nursing schools.
5. She wants to reach her goal in ten years.

Lesson F: Another view pages 34–36

A

1. $85
2. Tuesday and Thursday
3. 6:30–8:30 p.m.
4. Meena Roy

B

1. The 8:00 a.m. class meets on Monday, Wednesday, and Friday.
2. Section 03 meets in Room 221.
3. Ms. Williams does not teach on Monday, Wednesday, and Friday.
4. Ms. Porter teaches Section 04.

Unit 3: Friends and family

Lesson A: Get ready pages 37–39

A

1. trunk
2. hood
3. engine

B

1. picked up
2. went
3. bought
4. broke
5. called

C

Answers will vary.

Lesson B: What did you do last weekend? pages 40–42

A

1. stayed	7. fixed
2. bought	8. barbecued
3. ate	9. went
4. met	10. read
5. drove	11. studied
6. took	12. played

B

1. She read a book.
2. She bought groceries.
3. She met a friend.
4. She played soccer.

C

1A. Did Julie stay home last Sunday?
1B. Yes, she did.
2A. Did Julie buy groceries last Monday?
2B. No, she didn't.
3A. Did Julie meet a friend last Friday?
3B. No, she didn't.
4A. Did Julie play soccer last Saturday?
4B. Yes, she did.

D

Answers will vary.

Lesson C: When do you usually play soccer? pages 43–45

A

1. When does Angel usually eat dinner? at 6:00 p.m.
2. When did Angel eat dinner yesterday? at 7:30 p.m.
3. When does Suki usually go to the gym? before work
4. When did Suki go to the gym yesterday? after work
5. When do Arturo and Bonita usually study? at night
6. When did Arturo and Bonita study yesterday? in the morning

B

1A. does
1B. plays
2A. did
2B. ate
3A. did
3B. went
4A. does
4B. goes

C

1. do
2. did
3. do
4. did
Answers will vary.

Lesson D: Reading pages 46–48

A

1. do the dishes
2. do the laundry
3. make the bed
4. take a nap

B

1. What does Marie usually do on Thursday night? She cooks dinner for her parents.
2. What did she do first at home? First, she cleaned the house.
3. What did she do next? Next, she cooked.
4. What did she do at 6:30? She called her parents.

C

1. Marie left work early.
2. She went to the supermarket.
3. She bought groceries.
4. She went home.
5. She cleaned the house.
6. She cooked dinner.
7. She watched TV.
8. She waited for her parents.
9. She called her parents.

Lesson E: Writing pages 49–51

A

My name is Min. Yesterday, I had a big party at my house. First, I called my friends to tell them about the party. Next, I went shopping for food. At the party, we listened to music and ate good food. We had fun. Finally, I cleaned the apartment. Now, I'm tired!

B

1. Hi Eric,
2. I will be home late. Could you please make dinner?
3. First, cook the chicken.
4. Next, make some rice.
5. Finally, cut the vegetables.
6. Thank you! I will be home at 7:15 p.m.
7. See you soon!

C

Answers will vary.

Lesson F: Another view pages 52–54

A

1. $24
2. $69
3. 300
4. 600
5. $0.10

B

1. How many minutes come with Samir's plan? 300 minutes
2. How many minutes did Samir use this month? 320 minutes
3. How much is Samir's basic plan? $58
4. How much did Samir pay for additional minutes? $5

C

Answers will vary.

Unit 4: Health

Lesson A: Get ready pages 55–57

A

1. He is taking medicine.
2. He is holding an X-ray.
3. She is on crutches.
4. She has a headache.

B

1. Ali hurt his leg.
2. Ali needed an X-ray.
3. Ali's son is Rashid.
4. Ali has to stay at the hospital.
5. Noor will pick up Ali from the hospital.

C

Answers will vary.

Lesson B: What do I have to do? pages 58–60

A

1. Keep in refrigerator.
2. Shake well.
3. Take with food.

B

1. What does she have to do? She has to get an X-ray.
2. What does he have to do? He has to go to the hospital.
3. What do I have to do? You have to use crutches.

4. What do they have to do? They have to take their medicine.
5. What do we have to do? We have to see a doctor.

C

Doctor: You have the flu.
You: What do I have to do?
Doctor: You have to stay in bed for three days.
You: Oh, OK.
Doctor: Here's your prescription. You have to take it in the morning.
You: Do I have to keep this medicine in the refrigerator?
Doctor: No, you don't. But keep it out of reach of children.
You: I understand.
Doctor: Call me if you have any questions.

Lesson C: You should go to the hospital. pages 61–63

A

1 What should I do?
2. What should he do?
3. What should she do?
4. What should they do?

B

1. You should see a dentist.
2. You should rest.
3. You should take some aspirin.
4. You should get an X-ray.
5. You should stay in the shade.
Answers will vary for Advice (2) on page 63.

C

1. *You:* My leg hurts. What should I do?
   Friend: You should rest. You shouldn't walk. You should get an X-ray.
2. *You:* My mother doesn't feel well. What should she do?
   Friend: She should take a break. She shouldn't stay in the sun. She should drink lots of water.
   You: OK, I'll tell her.

Lesson D: Reading pages 64–66

A

1. allergies   4. rash
2. sprained   5. pressure
3. pains   6. cut

B

1. A	6. B
2. B	7. B
3. B	8. A
4. A	9. A
5. B	10. B

C

1. You shouldn't stand on the top step.
2. You should take this with food.
3. You should wear a tool belt.
4. You should keep this away from children.

Lesson E: Writing pages 67–69

A

1. I was at work. I picked up a heavy box. I hurt my back.
2. I was in my house. I fell off a ladder. I have a headache.
3. I was in the kitchen. I picked up a hot pan. I burned my hand.

B

1. What day did the accident happen? January 24, 2008
2. What time did the accident happen? 8:00 p.m.
3. What happened? Eduardo hurt his foot.
4. How did the injury happen? He slipped.

C

Employee name: Eduardo Perez
Date of accident: January 24, 2008
Time: 8:00 p.m.
How did the accident happen?: I was at work. There was water on the floor. I slipped and hurt my foot. I had to go to the hospital.

Lesson F: Another view pages 70–72

A

1. You should take this medicine for headaches, toothaches, colds, and backaches.
2. Children under 12 should take no tablets.
3. An adult should take one tablet at one time.
4. An adult can take six tablets in one day.

B

Down	Across
1. blood	3. chills
2. report	4. hospital
3. cut	6. tablet
5. label	

Unit 5: Around town

Lesson A: Get ready pages 73–75

A

1. departure board
2. waiting area
3. information desk
4. ticket booth
5. track number
The boxes spell "train."

B

1. What time does the train to Washington, D.C., leave? 9:00
2. What time does the train to Boston leave? 11:00
3. What time does the train to New York City leave? 10:00
4. What track does the train to Washington, D.C., leave from? Track 1
5. What track does the train to Boston leave from? Track 2

Lesson B: How often? How long? pages 76–78

A

1. How often does the bus go from York to City Airport? three times a day
2. How long does it take to get from York to City Airport? one hour and 40 minutes
3. How often does the bus go from City Airport to York? four times a day
4. How long does it take to get from City Airport to York? two hours and 10 minutes
5. What time does the 4:00 p.m. bus arrive at City Airport? 5:40 p.m.
6. What time does the 6:00 p.m. bus arrive in York? 8:10 p.m.

B

Answers will vary.

Lesson C: She often walks to school. pages 79–81

A

1. Ben never takes the bus to school.
2. Ben often drives to school.
3. Lenka rarely rides her bike to school.
4. Lenka usually takes the bus to school.
5. Sushila always rides her bike to school.
6. Sushila never drives to school.

B

1. Omar always comes to class.
2. He is rarely late.
3. He sometimes comes with his friend Paolo.
4. They usually take the bus.

C

Answers will vary.

Lesson D: Reading pages 82–84

A

1. write postcards
2. buy souvenirs
3. go sightseeing
4. stay at a hotel

B

1. How often do Miriam and her mother go on trips? They rarely go on trips.
2. When did they go shopping? They went shopping yesterday.
3. When do they want to go sightseeing? They want to go sightseeing tomorrow.
4. How long does the sightseeing bus trip take? It takes about three hours.

C

Answers will vary.

Lesson E: Writing pages 85–87

A

1. Where did Soledad go? She went to Canada.
2. Who did she visit? She visited her brother and his wife.
3. How often does she go there? She goes there twice a year.

4. How long does it take to get there? It takes five hours.
5. What did she do there? She visited Niagara Falls.

B

Answers will vary.

Lesson F: Another view pages 88–90

A

1. 18 minutes
2. twice a day
3. 13 minutes
4. three times
5. two

B

Unit 6: Time

Lesson A: Get ready pages 91–93

A

1. (a) Maria was born in 1982.
2. (d) Maria started school in 1987.
3. (e) Maria got her first job in 1998.
4. (b) Maria graduated from college in 2005.
5. (c) Maria got married in 2007.

B

Answers will vary.

Lesson B: When did you move here? pages 94–96

A

1. begin – began
2. finish – finished
3. have – had
4. get – got
5. find – found
6. graduate – graduated

7. leave – left
8. study – studied
9. meet – met

B

1. When did Amir leave India? In 1998.
2. When did Amir move to Los Angeles? In 2000.
3. When did Amir start college? In 2003.
4. When did Amir graduate from college? In 2006.
5. When did Amir meet Usha? In 2005.
6. When did Amir and Usha get married? In 2007.

C

Answers will vary.

Lesson C: He graduated two years ago. pages 97–99

A

1. in
2. on
3. at
4. on
5. in
6. in
7. at
8. on
9. on
10. in
11. in
12. on
13. on
14. in
15. at

B

1. Alicia started college in 2000.
2. Anton and Alicia got married in 2006.
3. Alicia graduated from college after she met Anton.
4. Alicia worked in an office before she started college.
5. Alicia graduated from high school in 1998.
6. Anton and Alicia got married before they moved to Argentina.

C

Answers will vary.

Lesson D: Reading pages 100–102

A

1. They fell in love.
2. They got engaged.
3. They got married.
4. They got a divorce.

B

1. studied
2. met
3. became
4. happened
5. took
6. moved

C

1. She immigrated in 1978.
2. She got promoted in 1980.
3. They became citizens after they got married.
4. They started a business after they moved to Chicago.

Lesson E: Writing pages 103–105

A

Gloria Estefan was born in 1957 in Havana, Cuba. She came to the United States in 1959. She started college in 1975. After she graduated, she became a singer with the Miami Sound Machine. In 1978, she married Emilio Estefan. They have two children. Her son was born in 1980. Her daughter was born in 1994. In 1990, Gloria was in a bus accident. She broke her back. She started to sing again in 1991. Her music is famous in many countries around the world. She also wrote books for children in 2005 and 2006.

B

1957: she was born
1959: came to the United States
1978: married Emilio
1980: son was born
1991: started to sing again
1994: daughter was born

C

1. Today is June 23. I graduated on June 20. I graduated three days ago.
2. It is 2008. I started my job in 2002. I started my job six years ago.
3. It is September 21. I started English classes on September 7. I started classes two weeks ago.
4. Today is Tuesday. I bought a car three days ago. I bought the car on Saturday.

Lesson F: Another view
pages 106–108

A

1. May 15, 1980
2. March 4, 1981
3. Lublin, Poland
4. Chicago, Illinois
5. April 7, 2008
6. April 5, 2008

Unit 7: Shopping

Lesson A: Get ready
pages 109–111

A

1. sofa
2. stove
3. customer
4. piano
5. salesperson

B

1. customer
2. salesperson
3. price tag
4. furniture
5. expensive

C

furniture: sofa, piano
appliances: stove
people: salesperson, customer
Answers may vary on page 111.

Lesson B: The brown sofa is bigger. pages 112–114

A

1. cheaper
2. bigger
3. more expensive
4. better
5. smaller
6. more comfortable
7. heavier
8. shorter
9. prettier
10. longer
11. taller
12. older

B

1A. Which car is older?
1B. Car a.
2A. Which car is smaller?
2B. Car b.

3A. Which sofa is more comfortable?
3B. Sofa a.
4A. Which sofa is prettier?
4B. Sofa b.
5A. Which table is cheaper?
5B. Table b.
6A. Which table is longer?
6B. Table a.

C

Answers will vary.

Lesson C: The yellow chair is the cheapest. pages 115–117

A

1. the friendliest
2. the nicest
3. the biggest
4. the best
5. the newest
6. the most expensive
7. the cheapest
8. the heaviest
9. the smallest
10. the most beautiful

B

1. Which TV is the cheapest? C
2. Which TV is the most expensive? A
3. Which TV is the largest? A
4. Which refrigerator is the cheapest? B
5. Which refrigerator is the most expensive? A
6. Which refrigerator is the heaviest? C

C

Answers will vary.

Lesson D: Reading pages 118–120

A

1. prettier
2. smallest
3. china cabinet
4. salesperson

B

1. What did Christine buy? Christine bought an entertainment center.
2. Why did Christine buy it? It's bigger.
3. What did Helen buy? Helen bought a recliner.

4. Why did Helen buy it? It's more comfortable.
5. What does Christine want to do now? Christine wants to watch TV all day.
6. What can Helen do now? Helen can relax after work now.

C

Answers will vary.

Lesson E: Writing pages 121–123

A

1. What is the best gift Tina ever received? The best gift she ever received was a bicycle.
2. Who gave it to her? Her father gave it to her.
3. Why did she receive it? It was for her tenth birthday.
4. Where did the gift come from? It came from the bicycle store near her home.
5. When did she receive this gift? It was a long time ago.
6. Why was it the best gift? She really needed it.
7. What happened to the gift? She gave it to her brother.

B

Answers will vary.

C

Answers will vary.

Lesson F: Another view
pages 124–126

A

1. the china cabinet
2. the refrigerator
3. the refrigerator and the stove
4. after 90 days
5. $1,960.00
6. $2,121.70

B

1. Juan Ramos
2. Bob Johnson
3. 8.25%
4. 32 Greenview Road, El Paso, Texas
5. 4141 Dayton Road, El Paso, Texas

Unit 8: Work

Lesson A: Get ready
pages 127–129

A

t	r	e	w	y	u	i	k	j	p	c	d	x
l	o	h	s	p	l	a	t	l	a	o	f	r
i	f	l	u	n	v	r	o	c	t	w	t	y
n	a	i	p	l	a	t	p	h	i	o	e	a
e	w	e	p	u	c	o	r	d	e	r	l	y
n	e	f	l	a	b	e	r	s	n	k	c	l
s	b	r	i	s	x	b	i	g	t	e	v	m
c	w	h	e	e	l	c	h	a	i	r	b	n
r	b	o	s	r	o	d	w	a	l	k	e	r

B

1. The patient has a broken leg and needs a wheelchair.
2. The orderly is delivering linens.
3. She is using a walker.
4. He is giving some medical supplies to his co-worker.

Lesson B: Where did you go last night? pages 130–132

A

1. ate
2. made
3. cleaned
4. delivered
5. met

B

1. What did Angela do at 10:00? She went to a meeting.
2. What did Inez and Martin do at 8:30? They took the linens to the eighth floor.
3. What did Inez and Martin do at 9:00? They prepared rooms on the sixth floor.
4. What did Angela do at 10:30? She picked up X-rays.

C

Answers will vary.

D

Answers will vary.

Lesson C: I work on Saturdays and Sundays. pages 133–135

A

1. Miguel takes the bus to work or rides his bike.

2. He goes to meetings, but he doesn't take notes.
3. He delivers mail and makes copies.
4. He answers calls, but he doesn't take messages.
5. He eats lunch in the cafeteria or at his desk.
6. He goes home after work or visits a friend.

B

Answers will vary.

C

Answers will vary.

Lesson D: Reading pages 136–138

A

Down
1. housewife
4. cashier
6. cook

Across
2. orderly
3. assistant
5. mechanic

B

1. Who wrote the letter? Denise Stephens wrote the letter.
2. What is Fernanda's job? She is a dental assistant.
3. When did she start? She started in 2005.
4. Why is she leaving? She wants to work closer to home.

Lesson E: Writing pages 139–141

A

1. Paolo works at Mom's Kitchen.
2. He was a cook.
3. He serves food and talks to customers.
4. He cleared tables.
5. He worked at Tito's Cantina.

B

Interviewer: What is your job?
Chisako: I am an orderly.
Interviewer: Where do you work?
Chisako: I work at South City Hospital.
Interviewer: What are your duties?
Chisako: I help the nurses and the doctors. I prepare rooms for the patients and meet patients in the reception area. I also pick up and deliver X-rays and medical supplies.

Interviewer: What job did you have before?

Chisako: I was a cashier.

Interviewer: Where did you work?

Chisako: I worked at Lucky's Supermarket.

Lesson F: Another view

pages 142–144

A

1. What is Ellen's hourly rate? $8.50
2. When did she start work on Thursday? 4:00 p.m.
3. When did she leave work on Tuesday? 11:00 p.m.
4. What day did she start work at 5:30 p.m.? Friday
5. How long is her dinner break? 30 minutes
6. What is the total number of hours she worked this week? 30.5

B

1. Can I give you a hand?
2. I can't make up my mind.
3. No, it was a lot of junk mail.
4. No, it was a piece of cake.

Unit 9: Daily living

Lesson A: Get ready

pages 145–147

A

1. lightbulb
2. garbage
3. washing machine
4. dishwasher

B

1. Mrs. Chan's washing machine was leaking.
2. Mrs. Chan's neighbor saw water under the door.
3. The neighbor called the building manager.
4. The building manager called a plumber.
5. The plumber came and fixed the leak.
6. Mrs. Chan thanked her neighbor the next day.
7. Mrs. Chan was very happy.

Lesson B: Which one do you recommend? pages 148–150

A

1. Helping Hands is insured.
2. Handy Repair Service is more experienced.
3. Helping Hands is cheaper.
4. Handy Repair Service takes credit cards.
5. Handy Repair Service is open 24 hours a day.

B

1. Which plumber do you recommend?
2. Which supermarket do you like?
3. Which bank do you recommend?
4. Which department store do you suggest?

C

Answers will vary.

Lesson C: Can you call a plumber, please? pages 151–153

A

1. fix the window
2. change the lightbulb
3. clean the floor
4. fix the toilet
5. unclog the sink

B

1. Would you repair the dishwasher, please?
2. Can you repair the stove, please?
3. Could you fix the lock, please?
4. Will you fix the dryer, please?
5. Could you call an electrician, please?
6. Can you unclog the sink, please?

C

Yes: Sure.; I'd be happy to.; No problem.; Of course.

No: Sorry.; I can't right now.; I'm busy.; Maybe later.

Lesson D: Reading pages 154–156

A

1. jammed
2. stained
3. cracked
4. bent

B

1. The tenant in Apartment 305 has a broken window.
2. There is a leaking washing machine in the laundry room.
3. The hall on the second floor has a burned-out light.
4. The sink is clogged in Apartment 203.
5. The tenant in Apartment 408 has a jammed door.

C

1. Could you call a repair person, please?
2. Could you change the lightbulb, please?
3. Could you call a plumber, please?
4. Could you fix the window, please?
5. Could you fix the back door, please?

Lesson E: Writing pages 157–159

A

April 10, 2008

Dear Building Manager,

I am a tenant at 469 W. Main St. I am writing to you about problems in my apartment. I am very upset. The ceiling is leaking water. The washing machine and dryer are broken. The window is also cracked. Could you please send a repair person right away? You can contact me in Apartment 2C if you have any questions. Thank you for your attention.

Sincerely,

Armen Krikorian

B

1. April 10, 2008
2. the building manager
3. a tenant / Armen Krikorian
4. problems in the apartment

C

1. date
2. opening
3. body
4. closing
5. signature

Lesson F: Another view
pages 160–162

A

1. How much did it cost to fix the dryer? $80
2. What was cracked? the window
3. Which repair was the most expensive? the door
4. Which repair was the cheapest? the window
5. How much is the total? $288

B

1. a locksmith
2. a plumber
3. a carpenter
4. a painter
5. an electrician

Unit 10: Leisure

Lesson A: Get ready
pages 163–165

A

Across	Down
1. perfume	1. party
3. card	2. flowers
5. balloons	4. cake
6. present	

B

1. party
2. balloons
3. cake
4. card
5. perfume
6. flowers

C

Answers will vary.

Lesson B: Would you like some cake? pages 166–168

A

1A. Would they like some cake?
1B. Yes, they would.
2A. Would she like a cup of tea?
2B. Yes, she would.

3A. Would he like a bottle of water?
3B. Yes, he would.
4A. Would you like some dessert?
4B. No, thank you.
5A. Would you like some soda?
5B. No, thank you.

B

1. I'd like some cheese.
2. He'd like some fruit.
3. She'd like a piece of pie.
4. They'd like some cookies.

Lesson C: Tim gave Mary a present. pages 169–171

A

1. Tito bought Mary some flowers.
2. Allie and Claire sent Harry a letter.
3. Lucia gave John some books.
4. Kong brought Yoshi and Naomi some cookies.

B

1. Tito bought her some flowers.
2. Allie and Claire sent him a letter.
3. Lucia gave him some books.
4. Kong brought them some cookies.

C

1. Susana likes them.
2. Claudia and Lorenzo like her.
3. Claudia likes him.
4. Lorenzo likes them.

Lesson D: Reading pages 172–174

A

1. Thanksgiving
2. Mother's Day
3. Valentine's Day
4. baby shower
5. New Year's Eve
6. housewarming

B

1. When was Denise's birthday party? last Saturday
2. Who came to the party? her classmates and relatives
3. Who gave her flowers and perfume? her grandparents
4. Who brought food and drinks? her mother
5. What did Denise's sister give her? a book
6. What did Denise do after the party? She wrote thank-you notes.

Lesson E: Writing pages 175–177

A

1. What did Mrs. Kramer give Mario? a backpack
2. What did his relatives give him? a dictionary
3. Why did Mario like the backpack? He liked the color.
4. Why did Mario like the dictionary? It will help him in English class.
5. When did he write the thank-you notes? on March 23, 2008

B

Answers will vary.

Lesson F: Another view
pages 178–180

A

1. The shower is for Ana Maria Garcia.
2. Michelle Wassem and Lois Smith are giving the party.
3. People need to say *yes* or *no* by May 21.
4. The party is on June 3.

B

Answers will vary.

Illustration credits

Denny Bond: (*bottom*) 10, 11, 12, 19, 20, 21, 46, 47, 48, 64, 65, 66, 91, 92, 93, 112, 113, 114, 133, 151, 152, 153

Roger Audette: 4, 5, 6, (*top*) 10, 11, 12, 25, 26, 27, 55, 56, 57, 82, 83, 84, 94, 95, 96, 109, 110, 111, 121, 122, 123, 145, 146, 147

Willie Ryan: 37, 38, 39, 58, 59, 60, 79, 80, 81, 115, 116, 117, 118, 119, 120, 154, 155, 156, 166, 167, 168

William Waitzman: 1, 2, 3, 13, 14, 15, 28, 29, 30, 49, 50, 51, 67, 68, 69, 73, 74, 75, 100, 101, 102, 127, 128, 129, 163, 164, 165, 172, 173, 174

Notes

Notes

Notes

Notes

Notes

Notes